I AM FUNNY LIKE THAT

HELEN C. ESCOTT

I AM FUNNY LIKE THAT

HELEN C. ESCOTT

ENGEN BOOKS

Published in Canada by Engen Books, St. John's, NL.

Library and Archives Canada Cataloguing in Publication

Title: I am funny like that / Helen C. Escott.
Names: Escott, Helen C., author.
Description: Previously published in 2016.
Identifiers: Canadiana (print) 20210102969 | Canadiana (ebook) 20210103108 | ISBN 9781774780060
(softcover) | ISBN 9781774780077 (PDF)
Subjects: LCSH: Escott, Helen C—Anecdotes. | CSH: Authors, Canadian (English)—21st century—
Anecdotes. | CSH: Women authors, Canadian (English)—21st century—Anecdotes. | LCGFT: Anecdotes.
Classification: LCC PS8609.S36 Z46 2021 | DDC C818/.602—dc23

Distributed by:
Engen Books
www.engenbooks.com
submissions@engenbooks.com

First mass market paperback printing: January 2016
Second mass market paperback printing: March 2021

Cover Image: Nate Gates https://nateandnicolephoto.com

To my husband Robert,
our children: Sabrina, Daniel, Colin,
my daughter-in-law Alanna
and grandchildren Sophie and Maximus.

Nora Ephron (a writer I admire) once said,
'Everything is copy.'

Well, that gives me permission to write about your childhoods and my mistakes. (In my defence I was trying to work full time, raise a family, keep a marriage together and clean the house. Judge me when you are my age.)

Love forever and always,
Mom

CONTENTS

PREAMBLE

In 2012 I started a blog called "I am Funny Like That." It had over 220,000 hits and many readers told me I should turn it into a book. So here it is! I am incredibly proud of this collection of short stories and snapshots of my daily family life.

"I am Funny Like That" describes my personality on many levels. I try to make people laugh every day and I am also a little weird in my ways. I hope you will see some similarities in our lives and these stories make you laugh out loud. Maybe you will find out you are funny like that, too.

Helen

Cover photo credits: Thank you Nate Gates NateAndNicolePhoto.com for putting this excellent photo together for the front of my book. I think you have captured my soul!

Thank you to my niece Brittany Hanlon for letting me have her beautiful baby girl, Brielle Smith, for the photo-shoot. She is a true diva just like her great-aunt Helen!

Thank you to my loyal companion, Minnie who just wandered onto the set and was included in the photo.

GRANNY PANTIES

For the record, I do not wear granny panties!

They are a nylon-spandex with reinforced tummy control panel support shaping panty that are engineered to hide the fact that I have given birth twice and keeps me from having muffin belly! I have more technology in my jeans than NASA has on the Space Shuttle.

I am cleaning out my underwear drawer and hubby tells me to throw out the "granny panties." To my horror I inform him, "I don't wear granny panties!" pointing out that my undergarments are carefully divided into my everyday comfortable nylon-spandex tummy controllers, my full-body Spanx that I wear under dresses, the panties that do not show through my dress pants and the foolishness he buys me every Christmas. There are no granny panties in this drawer!

He picks up a pair of my NASA engineered favourites and insists, "These are granny panties."

"No, they are not!" I protest, "Granny panties are cotton, with flowers all over them and come up to your armpits." I grab my daily favourites out of his hand, "These are a modern-day wonder! They hide years of not doing sit-ups every day, cellulite dimples, Big Macs with extra sauce and muffin belly! My grandmother never had panties like this!"

"Call them what you want. They are modern-day granny panties," he informs me.

Putting them back in the drawer I think, 'I would have to join a gym if I ever gave these beauties up.'

Anyway, it got me to thinking. I made a visit to a lingerie store. Maybe my underwear drawer did need some updating.

The walls of the store were lined with massive posters of girls who do not eat so they can wear lace without tummy control panels. Looking at their photoshopped abs did not inspire me to drop to the floor and do a hundred sit-ups, it just made me want to hold them down and force-feed them hamburgers.

The twenty-something salesgirl came over with her size zero figure and asked if I needed help. "I am looking to update my underwear drawer," I tell her. "I am looking for something that is comfortable but... sexy."

I know in her head she's thinking: "Sex at her age! Wow, good for her!"

First, she shows me the wall of underwear to turn on perverts. "No, that's not what I am looking for," and we move along to the "School girl" underwear to turn on pedophiles. "That's not me either," I tell her. Then she shows me the "new" line just in that week with the red or black fur around the waistband. "Doesn't that show through your dress pants?" I ask her. "Oh, you don't wear anything over these ones." That ought to make my workday more interesting, I think to myself.

Then she brings out the most dreaded, torturous device known to woman... the G-String!

I tried a pair once and I looked like a sumo wrestler. Even I laughed when I looked in the mirror. It brought back a memory to me. I was doing a two-day course at university. Before the course started the students were standing around the back of the class chatting and getting to know one another. I met this lovely lady who told me she was 60 years old and was doing the course out of interest. When it was time to sit down, she sat in front of me and to my horror she was wearing low-cut jeans that revealed a tattooed pair of eyes above her butt cheeks; but the worst part, she was wearing a silver thong.

It was like a car crash; I could not look away. For seven hours the droopy eyes on her butt watched me, staring at me, scarring me for life. Every time she put up her hand to ask a question her hips shifted, and her butt winked at me. The sliver G-string thread around her waist looked like a disco Hippie headband. I would never be able to look at a G-string without thinking of her butt eye balling me.

"I don't do fanny-floss," I told her. I need something comfortable. "Maybe you should go to Walmart," she said.

"Maybe you should go to hell," I thought.

With her sales commission still in my wallet, I left and called hubby from my cell phone in the car.

"Okay, I am willing to compromise. What would be your favourite underwear?"

"The ones that are on the floor," he confesses.

"I don't have to buy a G-string?"

"God no!" he says, to my great relief.

"I can keep my aerodynamically engineered control top undies?"

"As long as I'm the only one who sees them," he says.

"It's a deal." And with a muffin belly safely concealed behind my nylon-spandex control top, I go through the nearest drive-thru for a chocolate milkshake and drive home, savouring every last drop.

It goes to prove, when it comes to granny panties: it is what is on the inside that counts (the amount of spandex listed on the inside tag, that is)!

A FUNNY THING HAPPENED TO ME ON THE WAY TO THE DELIVERY ROOM

My mother got her wish, and I got a daughter just like myself.

I wanted a daughter since I was five years old. My very own living dolly. I knew exactly what she was going to look like. I knew the colour of her hair, her eyes and what she smelled like.

The day she was born the nurse put her in my arms and I knew I was right. Her face was familiar. She was everything I had dreamed of.

I went on a massive shopping spree. I bought dresses in every colour, tights with frilly bums and black patent leather shoes. I spent my days dressing and undressing her. Combing her hair into high pigtails, then French braids, and then the most perfect ringlets you have ever seen.

Then she turned two and learned the word "No."

"No comb hair, mommy!!!!"

No, no, no!!! Everything was "No" with ten exclamation points after it. By the time she was three she could hit notes that Celine Deon could only dream of, and every time I put a dress on her she would pull it up over her head like cone.

She had a mind of her own and strong opinions on

everything. My mother would say to me, "You're making too much out of her! You're spoiling her." But I did not know how to make any less of her. How do you not spoil your only little girl?

If you think I am bad at not spoiling her you should meet her father! This once fierce drill Sergeant who could make grown men shake in their boots with a single look is powerless against her pout. His yell would make both of our sons run to their rooms in fear but barely makes her blink. A simple hug from her and money becomes no option for him.

Next month, she turns twelve. She has become more beautiful than I could possibly imagine. She has the most amazing capacity to love. No one could love the life out of a teddy bear like she can. Her sights are now set on the latest boy band and her dreams of growing up to marry one of them brings me back to the days when I plastered posters of the Bay City Rollers on my bedroom wall and swore I would marry Lesley. Every night she rearranges her first best friend, second best friend, and third best friend (depending on the day's activities).

She has been known to throw a few shopping mall tantrums. I have heard the phrase "Please mom, why can't I have it?" or "I'm the only one who doesn't have one!" more than once. Where have I heard those words before? Every time she makes her dying plea for the latest, greatest object of her affection I think back to my own mother and what I put her through.

In my day, I have been known to throw a few Woolworth tantrums, myself. My parents separated when I was five years old. My mother was a single parent with ten children and ran a boarding house. She worked her fingers to the bone. Looking back now, I do not know how she ever did it. Someone once asked my brother if he remembered what he got for Christmas when he was a child, and he responded, "Another brother or sister!"

I remember stomping off at the Arcade on Water Street with my arms folded in pure defiance and my bottom lip stuck out because I wanted something and she said no. I often say to my daughter, "There's not a tantrum you can throw that I haven't already mastered."

My mother would always give in just as I do.

In the end my mother's wish came true, I got a daughter just like myself. I guess we do all become our mothers eventually, and we have daughters like ourselves.

It is funny, I spent the first half of my life desperately trying not to become my mother, and now I am spending the second half of my life desperately hoping to become half the woman that she is.

Here is hoping my daughter has a daughter just like herself someday, too.

CRACK DEALERS IN THE HOOD!

My doorbell rings one morning and my dog loses her mind, as usual. I am not expecting anyone; I look out through the glass door to see a big, husky man standing there with a stack of paper in his hand.

Avoiding my inner voice that's screaming "Don't open the door! You are home alone! You are in a housecoat! You could be murdered!" I open the door to a complete stranger while standing there in my housecoat because *that is what polite women do.* We would rather people say, "Too bad she opened the door to a stranger and was murdered," than "She wouldn't open the door and was SO rude!" We would not want to offend anyone. Especially by passing judgment on a big, husky man who could easily overpower us.

Turns out this big, husky man (who I could now see was dressed in painting clothes) was a crack dealer and wanted to know if I was interested in buying some crack from him.

I politely told him no, that I already had a crack dealer I had been using for years. He then asked me to take a flyer just in case I became unhappy with my crack dealer and wanted a new one or had a friend who was looking for a good crack dealer. I told him sure, and I politely took his crack flyer and closed the door, but waited until he got to the end of the driveway before I locked it, because I did not want him to think I thought he was a murderer.

Well actually, he was not selling crack. He was selling home repairs.

When I opened the door my dog, who had been losing her mind (who obviously had better safety instincts than me and didn't care about being rude) ran out the door and circled the guy's feet while barking loud enough to alert the neighbours that a killer was in the neighbourhood. The man, in a feeble attempt to prove that he was not a murderer bent down to rub my dog.

That is when his true intent was exposed! The crack!

His paint-covered jeans pulled all the way down to the bottom of his hairy crack and his too-short T-shirt rose all the way up his waist. All I could do was stand there in my house coat, frozen, unable to look away and feeling my morning coffee rising in my throat until I realized I had just thrown up in my mouth!

Being a lady, who is never impolite, I swallowed the regurgitated coffee and continued to have a conversation with this man about dealing crack, or home renovations, in my neighbourhood.

He started fast-talking me about his expertise with drywall, plastering, and painting, but all I could think about was that crack! I knew that I could not spend weeks, days or even an hour knowing that every time he bent down to pick up a tool I would be exposed to crack.

Then I had to think of my poor dog. He does like to lick everything. I could never let him kiss me again! I mean sure, I do not mind him smelling another dog's butt at the park, but crack is whack! He may never go back!

I took the flyer and put it in the recycling can and figured it was the last of this crack dealer. That was, until the next day when I was getting into my truck. The dog started losing her mind again. I had to chase her to the end of the driveway and grab the dog by the collar to settle her down.

Then I noticed it... the crack was back!

There it was across the street laying fence palings on my neighbour's lawn. She had hired the crack dealer to fix her fence!

I was transfixed. I had to slow down and look. The crack was smiling back at me. From stem to stern!

The crack was back and smack in my tracks!

I had hoped by the time I came home that day her fence would be fixed, and the hood would be back to normal.

Turns out she was running a crack house across the street.

After the fence, he painted her garage door, then there was work on the inside of her house as well. Apparently, my neighbour has a crack problem.

Every time I left my house or came home, I had a crack attack.

She must have eventually been forced into rehab by her husband because the crack dealer was gone after a week.

I was leaving my house this morning when I heard her call out to me. She was leaving for work and was waving hello. I could not help but ask, "Got all your renovations finished?"

"Yes," she answered. "I hired a local handyman. He took a long time to get the job done and his work was kind of sloppy. I wouldn't recommend him."

"Good to know," I smiled back at her.

Turns out in the end, our crack dealer was not all he was cracked up to be!

ARE MEN THE NEW WOMEN?

When my daughter was turning eight years old, I booked a mother-daughter pedicure at a local salon as a treat. She had been excited all week and when the day came, she could barely contain herself. We walked into the treatment room at the beauty salon and were both a little shocked to see the only other client in the room was a man in his fifties. He was obviously uncomfortable to see us as well.

I have nothing against a man getting a pedicure. As a matter fact, I think it is a great idea. It should be mandatory for all men to get pedicures. Especially at the beginning of summer before they wear sandals, so it does not look like someone went at their feet with a chainsaw or, even worse, like they have two-inch-long claws. But I must admit, I am not fussy about men invading the only place women have left to get away from them.

I smiled and said Hello. Realizing that he was uncomfortable, I decided to go about my business and get my pedicure. My daughter, on the other hand, was fascinated by this man in a woman's world. She literally stood there, staring at him with her mouth wide open. The more she stared, the more he squirmed.

I quickly lifted her onto the pedicure chair, hoping

that would distract her. As soon as she settled down, she began to stare again.

I tried everything I could to distract her. I offered her magazines. I offered her my phone to play with. I tried talking to her. It would only distract her for a few seconds, then her eyes would go back to this poor man and she would stare with her mouth open like a busybody at an accident scene.

This eight-year-old little girl had this man in his fifties squirming like he was in an interrogation chair. He could not have been more uncomfortable if she had walked into a change room at a lingerie store and caught him trying on a lace garter and bra. Luckily, he was nearing the end of his pedicure and the lady was doing the final file on his toenails.

I looked at my daughter and knew the wheels were turning in her little brain. Just like the slow-motion section of a movie, I could see her lips about to form a word but before I could intercept, she asked the man, "What colour polish are you getting? I'm getting Princess Pink!"

The man smiled at her and said, "I am not getting a colour."

Then, to make sure this man never returned to the inner sanctum of female-hood, she delivered the death blow: "My dad would never get a pedicure, he says it's too girly for him."

The poor man smiled and ran out of there like he had been caught with a hooker by his wife.

I have never seen another man in the pedicure room since. I am sure he told all his friends, and they told their friends so none of them will ever take the chance of coming up against my eight-year-old daughter in a beauty salon.

Just a little while ago I was at the beauty salon getting my hair dyed back to its natural red (don't laugh). In the next chair was a man in his late forties or early fifties. He was also wearing the hair-dye cape. Personally, I think men look extremely sexy when they start to turn grey. I assumed this guy was getting rid of his. To my shock, the hairdresser pulled out the cart with all the rollers on it and proceeded to put them in his hair. He was getting a perm!

It took everything I had to not scream at him: "No one gets perms anymore!" Followed by: "Do I need to tell you why you're not wearing a wedding band?"

I could not help but overhear the conversation between him and his hairdresser. He shared that he was newly divorced and wanted to update his look. Now why she allowed this poor, misguided man to get a perm was beyond me. She obviously had an ex-husband she hated. When the time came to take out the rollers and wash out the perm the poor man looked like he had a Brillo pad on his head.

He got out of the chair and noticed me staring at him.

With a smile and a wink, he joked, "Too bad you're wearing that wedding ring, because I would've asked for your number."

I just smiled and said, "Oh, too bad for me." Thinking in my head, "I am holding out for the hottie with the comb-over two chairs down."

It got me to thinking... why are men wandering into female territory? Then a friend told me these men are "Metrosexual." According to the internet, a metrosexual man has taste and knows about fashion, art, and culture. He appreciates the finer things in life and enjoys making himself look good through styling his hair or wearing fashionable clothes. For example, men who cannot walk past Winners without buying a designer label for less. Or men who own twenty pairs of shoes, half a dozen pairs of sunglasses, and carry a man-purse. Or if he sees a stylist instead of a barber because barbers do not do highlights, then he is a metrosexual man.

I love when a man takes care of himself. They can all do with a little manscaping on top and below. It is wonderful that they are learning how to dress. How many times have you seen men walking around in the summertime wearing black dress socks with sandals? Or even worse, when the sandals have Velcro closures. How about the guy who still wears the black velvet blazer he wore to his prom thirty years ago? Or the guy whose tie ends in the middle of his chest? It is about time men took an interest in their hair. Ask any man if you can see his kindergarten picture and even though he may be in his forties, I bet he still has the same haircut!

I think it is great that men are trying new things.

One time I tried to introduce my husband to the spa world. I booked a full day of pampering for the two of us. He loved the couples' massage. The trouble came when we went for body wraps.

We were put in separate rooms that were about ten feet away from each other. First, they scrubbed us down with sea salt to exfoliate the body. They rinsed it off with warm soapy water and massaged oil all over our bodies. We were wrapped in warming blanket like mummies. The attendants told each of us we had to lay there and relax for about forty minutes for the process to work properly and they would be back to wake us when the time was up.

It only took about five minutes before I heard my husband snoring. As the minutes went by the snoring got louder, until the amplified sound of it filled the entire floor.

I called out several times for an attendant to come back, but they had obviously gone for their break. I wanted to tell one of them to roll him on his side to stop the snoring, but no one could hear me. I tried to free my hands, but the wrap was too tight. I considered rolling off the table and jumping down to his room to wake him, but I was constrained like a mental patient.

For forty minutes I lay thinking of all the ways I would kill him when I was freed. The attendants finally returned. My husband said he had the best sleep of his life. I, on the other hand, was stressed to the max and my blood pressure was about twenty points higher than what it should have been. I vowed never to take him to a spa again.

When I think of a man, I think of John Wayne or Tom Selleck. I like a man with a hairy chest and a moustache. I hate skinny men. I want a man with some meat on his bones, something to cuddle into. Now I am not saying I like a man with a "dicky-do (his stomach sticks out more than his dicky do), or a muscleman. Just a nice soft place to land.

I like a man's hands when they are rough and not soft like a woman's hands. I do not want a man who smells nicer than me, has more hair products than me, or looks better than me. When we go out on the town, I want people to see me first, not him! I want to be the star attraction. I am the one who had to dilate ten centimetres, twice! And squeeze a head the size of a grapefruit out of a hole the size of a grape! I deserve the spotlight after a day of waxing, shaving, makeup, and an hour on my hair. Which is done while I make sure the kids eat their supper, pick up the babysitter, *and* find his keys, tie-clip, and underwear.

I do not want to turn grey, but I think it is sexy when a man does. I know it is a double standard: when a man goes grey, he gets distinguished, when a woman goes grey, she gets replaced. But I think men look better as they age. I think women like the Neanderthal man more than the metrosexual man. Now it would be great if Neanderthal man had a pedicure every now and then and did not leave skid marks on his boxers. But maybe it is a slippery slope.

Maybe once they get a taste of pampering, they cannot stop.

I like to think that I am a modern woman and as a woman I know we have fought for decades to have equality in a man's world. Now I have to wonder, can we return the favour and allow men to have equality in a woman's world?

Will a man ever be able to have a pedicure without having to dodge looks from the eight-year-old girls in the room? Or get a perm without a woman giggling behind his back? Will a man ever feel truly equal in a woman's world?

It may seem selfish, but I do not want men to be equal in our world. I own eighty percent of our closet, and I am not giving it up! I am also not giving up one inch of the bathroom counter and I am definitely not bringing my husband to my next pedicure appointment. That is my time to relax and be pampered without someone asking me "What's for supper?" or "How much is this costing us?"

Are men the new women? Maybe. But if most of their gender thinks Velcro sandals with black dress socks are a good fashion move, we will not have to worry about losing our pedicure chairs to them anytime soon.

ANGELS WE HAVE HEARD ON HIGH

Did you know 68% of Americans believe in angels? I am not surprised.

Most of us believe in some kind of angel. Whether it is the Biblical kind that appears to George Bailey in *It's a Wonderful Life* or a Victoria Secret Angel (although they are not real angels, they are photoshopped). Maybe it is just someone who guided you or helped you at some point in your life.

I have always believed that angels come to you when you ask them to and in many forms. Sometimes human and sometimes animal. I think when someone steps into your life and changes the course you are on for the good, they are an angel. These deeds may not always be earth-shattering deeds that open the heavens. They could be a small gesture or a word.

When I was young, I was a tomboy. No one really knew I was a girl until I was about sixteen! Let's just say I was a little homely. I was also painfully shy, so I was not good at holding a conversation either. A friend of my family was visiting from the mainland. At supper he tried his best to include me in the conversation but the best I could do was a nod or say "yup." He must have grown frustrated at one point because he looked me in the eye and said, "You know, Helen, if you would learn to talk properly you could really go places. I know you have interesting things to say. So just say them. I'd like to hear your opinion."

It was the first time anyone had asked me for my opinion. His words stuck with me for the rest of my life. Every time I was too shy to speak up, I kept hearing: "I know you have interesting things to say. So just say them." That one comment changed the course of my life. I taught myself to speak up and remembered that what I had to say mattered. He was an angel.

Over the years I have been involved with a youth organization focused on girls and I have done several career talks to teens. I always seek out that one kid that stands in the back of the room or hides in the corner. I find something nice to say that will make them feel good about themselves. Like, "I loved that picture you painted. You're such a good artist." Or "You're so smart. Tell me what you are going to be when you finish school."

I see myself in that kid and I make sure I pay it forward. I realized that one good, encouraging comment you say to a kid may be the one that changes their whole life. You may be their angel.

When I finished high school, I knew I wanted to go into broadcasting. No one in my family had gone to university or done any post-secondary education. I found university intimidating. I called Student Services one day and tried to explain what I wanted to do but the person on the other end of the phone did not have the motivation or time to help me. I became discouraged and was ready to give up. I just did not know how to say out loud: "I want to be in broadcasting now help me!"

My friend Carol, who had a car at the time, which was

a big thing, because I could barely afford the bus, told me, "I will pick you up tomorrow and drive you to the university and we will find the program that's right for you." She did and we found a broadcasting course in Edmonton that I liked. She helped me apply and I got in. The rest, as they say, "Is history." I graduated, went into broadcasting, then jumped to communications. Carol was an angel who took the time to help a friend and it changed the course of my life.

In 2012 I had back surgery. The surgeon removed three discs in my lower back and installed two titanium rods and eight screws. The recovery was brutal. I had to learn to walk again. I started with a walker and worked my way up to a cane. I went to physio, worked with the doctor, and did everything I was told because I was determined I would walk without any assistance at all. The surgeon who fixed my back was definitely an angel but not the main one in this story.

The archangel was Minnie, my dog. She is a cross between a black Labrador Retriever and a Terrier. I got her as a puppy from a lady who advertised "free puppies" on the internet.

Minnie wanted to go outside to pee at least ten times a day. She wanted to play and continuously brought me a tennis ball to throw. She wanted to go for walks around the block and refused to take no for an answer. Every day I forced myself off the couch to let her outside to pee. I sat on the back step and threw the ball to her. I tied her leash to my walker and dragged myself to the top of the street. Three months later I only needed my cane to get around. Getting up off the couch became easier. I could now stand and throw the ball and chase her to get it back. The walks became longer. Eventually I did not need the cane at all. I became convinced this mutt I got free on the internet was indeed a furry angel.

I still have back pain and I sometimes find it hard to get around. It always astonishes me when I am lying in bed dealing with my pain how Minnie jumps up and lays next to me. Right where the pain is. Like she knows. It's like she lays her invisible wing over my pain and says "I am here, mom. You're not alone."

We have become a world of people who look up to celebrities. I read one statistic that said one out of every three young girls would rather be famous than intelligent. That is startling considering many women in third world countries do not have the right to be educated let alone famous.

I have never idolized a celebrity. I have plastered my bedroom with posters of Elvis and the Bay City Rollers back in the day because I loved their music, but I never wanted to be like them. Back then we also did not know every move celebrities made like we do today.

Can you imagine if Elvis sent out a Tweet every time he moved? The whole internet would be all shook up!

There are too many so-called celebrities misguiding young people. It is too easy to find the anti-angels.

Angels do walk among us. They are everyday people, and animals, who just happen to be in the right place at the right time in your life. They motivate you to think about your life, they inspire you to do something, they put their arms (and paws) around you and comfort you when you need it. They give you hope. They create serendipity – the happy accident.

Whether you believe in God or not, you have to believe in angels. Think about your life and the people who changed it for the better: they are the Angels you have heard on high.

FIFTY SHADES OF GREY - OR, MY VERSION FOR THOSE FORTY AND OVER, 'FIFTY WAYS A DAY.'

I have read all three books: *Fifty Shades of Grey, Fifty Shades Darker,* and, *Fifty Shades Freed.* I liked it. It is not Shakespeare but E.L. James doesn't claim to be Shakespeare. Neither do I. I think we would be good friends.

The book glamorizes sexual deviancy the way *Pretty Woman* glamorized prostitution. Remember when Julia Roberts played a prostitute and Richard Gere played the rich John. They fell in love and then every girl in her twenties wanted to be a prostitute because of the glamorous lifestyle.

We all know how glamorous prostitutes have it.

It is the same old story.... poor unknowing virgin meets insanely rich man. She manages to do what no other woman before her could... fix him and make him happy!

Bla! Why is it never the other way around? Why is it never the poor unknowing male virgin meets the rich beautiful woman? Why is it women never gets to be on top?

It is a good read if you are in your twenties or thirties. If you are in your forties or fifties, you will just want to bitch-slap the lead character Anastasia Steele and say, "Smarten up!"

It got me to thinking. I am a writer! I could write a

book like this for women in their forties and up! Soft porn for women going through the change! I am fiftyish. I know what turns on a woman going through mid-life. I sat at my computer and began my erotic, amusing and deeply moving "Fifty Ways a Day" a tale that will obsess you, possess you and stay with you forever.

Chapters 1- 9

These chapters suck because you are just getting to know the characters. Skip to Chapter 10 where the good stuff happens.

Chapter 10

Christian Ways, the Adonis, stands in my kitchen. His tool belt hanging off his hips, the way I like it. I am the richest woman in the world and this poor carpenter has responded to my ad in the newspaper for a "Handyman." I warn him, there is a contract he will have to sign.

He says he is into vanilla carpentry. No add-ons, no toys. My dog walks into the kitchen. "Who's that?" he questions. "That's Charlie Tango, my dog. Get used to him." He seems impressed.

"What do you want me to do for you?" he asks shyly. I stare down at my knotted fingers. "There's a hole in my wall. Do you know how to fill it?" I question him. "I have Fifty Ways of fixing everything." I gasp at his assertiveness.

His gaze is unwavering and intense. His tousled hair falls on his face, his voice is like dark melted chocolate fudge caramel. The kind you can only get in those Cadbury eggs at Easter.

"You should steer clear of me. I am not the handyman for you," he warns. "Fix my wall," I order him. He is home improvement on legs, I think to myself.

He moves gracefully through the kitchen. His muscular arm reaches to the top of the wall and he slides his hand down, feeling the texture. He examines the hole. "I can fix this hole now." Without warning he whips out a trowel from his tool belt. It sends shivers down my spine. Where did the plaster come from? I do not know. Within seconds the hole is filled and the smell of plaster and sweat is intoxicating. "What now?" he greedily asks me.

"There's a hissing in my toilet. It's been there for weeks."

"Show me to the bathroom," he orders, and I oblige immediately. Before I know it, he is on his knees... listing to the hiss. "I know how to stop your hiss," he tells me. I stand beside him, relishing his knowledge. Maybe he is too good for me. I have had three plumbers look at this toilet. Neither could find my hiss. His fingers carefully lift off the top of my toilet and sensually lay it on the closed seat. He plunges his hand into the cold toilet water. "It's wet," he says. "I know. The water in there always is," I warn him.

Fifty Ways knows his stuff. He whips out the hose. "Your hose is broken." He gently pulls a knife out of the tool belt.

It is still hanging on his hips. The way I like it. He cuts the hose and places it back in the cold, wet water. "Your hissing is gone now. I've cut out the broken part," he explains. "You don't need a long hose to get the job done. Sometimes a shorter hose can do that job, too."

He was just Fifty Ways of craziness. He bent over to pick up the toilet seat and his Levi's were as tight as the fitted sheet on my mother's bed.

"What's next?" He is brazened. My head is swimming. I did not expect it to be like this. Getting all this work done today. I quiver and gasp.

"My hardwood floors aren't level," I groan. "Show me," he commands.

I take him to the living room. He gets down on all fours. In an earth-shattering moment he pulls out his level. Oh my God. I had no idea my floors were that bad! It tears at my soul. I stare down at my knotted fingers then at Fifty. His grey eyes turn cold. He pulls something out of his pocket, and I hear the tearing of foil. I cannot believe it! He has his own steel wool!

"I can't fix this. I am not the handyman for you," he cries out. "I'll think about your contract and get back to you."

He does not smile. He just turns on his heels and stalks to the front door. "Good-bye," he softly says, and he looks utterly, utterly broken. A man in agonizing pain. I tear my gaze from him. The physical pain of losing him overtakes me and I surrender myself to my grief. "A good handyman is so hard to find," I cry out.

The end.

Stay tuned for book two. While the handyman wrestles with not being able to fix the floor, the richest woman in the world must confront the anger and envy of all the other women in the neighbourhood who want him to fix their holes.

IF I JUST HAD FIVE MORE MINUTES!

Sometimes I wonder if I got dropped repeatedly as a child. I just continue to do the most stupid things.

Over Christmas I left my ATM card in the machine at the grocery store and did not realize it till the next day when I went to pay for lunch at a restaurant. Luckily, I had a credit card in my wallet, or I would have been washing dishes that afternoon. I had to go to the bank to get a new one. You would think I learned a lesson, but I did the exact same thing again a day later! After paying for groceries, I went off and left the damn card in the machine again. Then I had to go back to the bank and admit that I needed another one.

Why am I in this constant state of confusion?

It is because I am so busy all the time. My whole life just needs five more minutes!

Rushing the kids out to the school bus. Waiting for the dryer to end so I can get another load in before I go to work. Drying my hair. If I just had five more minutes!!!

Multitasking is just a joke! Just this very minute while writing a report for work I Googled a recipe for chicken, wrote "Don't forget to pay for daughter's dance class" on a post-it note and attached it to my purse, and fixed the scuff on my high heels with a black marker. Then my mother phones to complain that I never call her anymore!

During a multitasking meltdown one morning, I was retrieving a message from my boss that he had left on my office phone, jotting down the information I needed to call him back with, while reading an email from my husband. I called my boss's office number and got his voice mail. While leaving him the information he needed, and answering the email back to my husband, I ended the message to my boss with "I hope that's all you needed. If not call me back. I love you. Bye" and hung up the phone.

I do not love my boss. He is okay. I like him but it is not love.

I realized what I did and ran like a woman on fire through the building to his office. He was not in yet, thank God, but his executive assistant was. I asked her if she had the code to his voicemail and told her what I did. She went in to retrieve the message, but it was not there.

"Maybe I didn't press the number to leave a message," I thought. Her phone rang and she picked it up. It was the boss. After a few pleasantries and the daily update, she tells him, "I am here with Helen now," jots down some info and hangs up the phone. "What did he say?" I ask, holding my breath. "He said to tell you he got your message and he's very fond of you, too."

As women we overtax ourselves. Trying to be a superwoman in stilettos. How many times has superwoman shown up at work with her skirt on backwards or wearing two different black shoes? I have.

My husband calls me every day to remind me to pick the kids up. I always say, "Do you really think I would forget?" Truth is, I always forget. Thank God he knows me better than I know myself.

Watch out if I have PMS on top of multitasking!

Hubby made the mistake of yelling at me from the basement to ask me where his white shirt was while I was trying to get a five-minute nap on the couch after supper.

Twice I yelled back that it was hanging in his closet. I know he can hear me, but he pretends he is deaf! I jumped off the couch and stomped to the basement door and screamed back, "You're not frigging deaf. While you are down there take the clothes out of the dryer and they better be folded before you come upstairs, or I'll kill you!" I slammed the door and stomped back to finish my five-minute nap.

What I did not know was that my husband was upstairs, not down in the basement.

The guy from heating company was in the basement fixing the furnace.

Hubby had let him in while I was upstairs helping the kids with homework twenty minutes earlier.

I did not know the heating guy was in the house until I heard a light tap on the living room door. I opened one eye to see the poor man standing there in his coveralls, holding a folded basked of laundry.

He said, "Missus, the furnace is fixed. You shouldn't have any problems now and the laundry is folded. I am not good at matching socks so you may want to check them." He laid the basket on the floor and slowly backed out of the room, then ran for his life.

I just needed five more minutes of sleep before starting the second half of my day; now the home heating guy thinks I am a maniac. I hope the furnace never breaks again because I know he is not coming back.

I think my brain is full and I cannot fit anything else in there. Every time I fill out a form for my kids I have to think, what year was my son born? I know we were married in '94; he was born two years later. It must be '96. No one will know if it is wrong anyway.

Do not even get me started on people's names. There are times I feel like lying to people and saying, "I had a stroke and lost my memory, so you'll have to remind me how I know you."

If I had five more minutes to think about it, I am fairly sure it still would not come to me.

BRINGING SEXY BACK WITH LINGERIE

I love my comfy nightdress. It is made from soft T-shirt material and has a round neck, so when I am eating chips in bed the crumbs never fall between my cleavage but bounce on the material and fall to the floor. That is important in a nightdress.

One night hubby made fun of my comfy nighty. I was a little put out by it really. He called it "A nightdress", "unsexy" and "old." I informed him, "This is sexy lingerie."

"A far cry from lingerie," he said.

I was insulted. I thought men liked it when women wore T-shirts to bed. Then I had to think... when did I buy this nightdress? It was about five years ago at a sale in the Gap at an outlet mall. Okay, maybe he was right. My favourite old nighty had to go.

The next day I went to Walmart and bought five new nightdresses. All very sexy lingerie, or so I thought. I was pleased with myself and my selection. That night I wore the first one, a little coral number with lace around the bottom. I walked into the bedroom, hand on my hip and said, "I bought lingerie. What do you think of this one?"

"That's not lingerie," he informed me. "That's a nightdress."

"No, it's not. It is lingerie. Look at the lace on the boobs, and it is coral! Coral is sexy!"

"It's nice but it's not lingerie and coral is not sexy."

"I bought five of these at Walmart today! All in different colours. Maybe the sky blue one is better."

"There's the problem. Lingerie doesn't come from Walmart," he told me.

Well, I was disgusted. When did coral stop being sexy? What about the lace covering my boobs? My God, have I forgotten what sexy is? Right there and then I decided to make it my mission to bring sexy back.

The next day I went to a lingerie store. I took my time and checked out every rack. A young salesgirl asked me if I needed any help. "Yes," I said, "I am on a mission to bring sexy back."

She looked at me with this weird "You're as old as my mother" look and said, "Anything in particular?"

"Yes. Lingerie."

"Oh," she said, obviously thinking I was some kind of cougar on the prowl. "This way." She led me to the back of the store where there were two racks of see-through, lacy, sparkly things on display. She pushed the hangers to one side and slid out a little silver, metallic number. "How about this one? This would look good on you," she lied.

It was a shiny chainmail bikini. The type of chainmail that knights in armour wear. Except no knight wore a chainmail bikini like this. Unless he was with the Knight's Village People. The bra part was made with two metal triangles and thin cubic zirconia straps that clasped in the back. The bottom was another metal triangle with a cubic zirconia G-string. I had to stare at it for a long time before my brain was able to even register what it was.

"Would you like to try it on?" she asked. My first

thought was, "How many women have tried it on already?" I do not see a protective panty liner on that cubic zirconia G-string. I wished I had kept a tin of Lysol Spray in my purse like my Mother did. I took it from her waiting hand, and it was surprisingly heavy. I trotted off into the change room.

I tried it on and stood back from the mirror. My first thought was, "Sure, I would freeze in this during the night. What if the window gets left open and the metal got cold? Hubby's tongue would get stuck to it. We'd have to call the fire department to rescue him." And where would the chip crumbs go? I would be kicked out of bed for eating chips!

Then I pictured my teenage daughter waking in the middle of the night calling out, "Mom, mom, I am sick!"

I would run to her room, grab the garbage bucket, and put it up to her face to catch the vomit before it hit the mattress. Then she would look up and see the metal bikini and think she was hallucinating, only to realize that she was not in the middle of some sick nightmare, but her mother really was standing in her room wearing a metal bikini made of triangles with cubic zirconias keeping it all together. The counselling would cost me thousands.

That is not the weirdest thought that came into my head though. What if one of those cubic zirconias came loose and worked its way up through me? I could end up in the doctor's office with my feet in stirrups, and just before she does the pelvic exam I would have to confess, "You may find a cubic zirconia in there... Just saying."

It started to itch, and I had to take it off. I could not sleep in that. It is too itchy. I put it back on the hanger and passed it back to the saleslady. "How was it?" she asked with a smile.

"Not for me," I tell her, waiting to see if she was going to spray the G-string part with sanitizer or Febreze or something else. She did not. "I think I'll keep looking."

I went down to Sears and found beautiful lingerie. It was made from soft T-shirt material, cozy and warm. It had "Sexy" written on the front of it. I figure if you cannot trust Sears who can you trust?

I bought my new "Sexy" lingerie and wore it that night. I pointed to my boobs. "It says sexy," I told hubby.

"Kind of inappropriate don't you think?" he asked.

"What?" What am I missing here? I asked myself.

"Going around the house with "sexy" wrote on your boobs! We have teenagers, you know?"

"But I thought you wanted sexy lingerie?" I was totally bewildered.

"I never said I wanted sexy lingerie. You told me your old nightdress was lingerie and I said it wasn't. I was not complaining. You finished that conversation in your head without me like you always do."

I tried to think back. Was it me or him? I could not remember.

Anyway, tomorrow I am bringing sexy back... right back to Sears and getting myself a proper nightdress.

Do you need a receipt to bring sexy back? Because I do not think I kept it. I may just have to donate "Sexy" to the Value Village.

DOES ANYBODY KNOW HOW TO BE A GOOD MOTHER?

I do not know what I am doing when it comes to being a mother. I have been winging it for years. I think my kids already figured that out.

There are hundreds, even thousands, of books on how to be a good mother. I have not read any of them. I have been too busy on the front lines of raising children to take the time out to read a book on how to do it properly.

I remember when my first child was born. After twelve hours of excruciating back labour and a nurse telling me to "Walk off the pain," I finally delivered a seven-pound baby boy. The nurse cleaned him off and placed my beautiful blue-eyed, naked son in my arms. I looked up at her, with wide eyed innocence and asked, "Why is he naked?" To which she responded with a laugh, "They don't come out with clothes on!" That should have been a clue to call child protective services.

That night, after my husband, mother and friends finally left, I was lying in my hospital bed, staring at this newborn baby wrapped up like a mummy in his glass bassinet. It was then I noticed he was also staring at me. We were both sizing each other up, wondering what to do next. I began to have a mini panic attack, thinking, "Who in their right mind would give me a baby? Don't they know I kill plants? I can't even remember to feed my cat every day!"

The next twenty years flashed before my eyes. Before I knew it, I was envisioning him getting married and moving out and he had not even come home yet. The craziest thoughts were bombarding my mind. Who would I trust with him? Who would I not trust with him? What if somebody tried to hurt him? What if he gets sick? Suddenly keeping him safe became the most important thing in my life. It still is.

Those first few months were quite a learning curve. I tried to be the Beaver Cleaver mother and Martha Stewart all rolled into one. It did not work out well. It turns out he was colicky, and I had postpartum depression. He cried. I cried.

I cried so much my husband banned the country music channel from our house because it would make me even more depressed.

Then one day my sister came to visit. My son was in the highchair, crying as usual, and I was trying to wash the kitchen floor, crying as usual. It seemed I could not do anything right. My normally spotless house was up to my ears, the breastfeeding was not working out, and I swear people in prison got more showers than me. I was afraid to admit to anybody that I was a failure.

That day my sister walked in and caught me crying in the mop bucket. She asked, "Did you take six months off to clean the house or to raise the baby?" She explained that nobody knows how to do this right; you make mistakes as you go and then you learn from them. Having a clean house should no longer be a priority. She told me if someone complains about how messy her house is, she says, "The vacuum is in the closet. Feel free to use it."

Then she gave me the best advice ever: "Everyone you meet will tell you how to raise a child. Especially people who do not have any. Before you take anyone's advice, look at their kids and ask yourself, do I want my kids to be like their kids? Then decide if you want to take their advice or not."

My mother always said never judge a person's success by the type of car they drive or the house they live in; judge their success by how their kids turn out.

Now that may not be fair either, because the mother gets the blame for everything. When my son was diagnosed with a nut allergy it was because I ate peanut butter when I was pregnant. If your kid has "issues" it is because we mother them too much. No one ever accuses men of "fathering" kids too much! It comes back to the old saying "The hand that rocks the cradle is the hand that rules the world."

As women it is in our nature to try and run everything. We all start out trying to be "Stepford Wives", those submissive and docile housewives who turn out to be robots created by their husbands, even though we are trying to climb the career ladder at the same time. Then we find out we are not robots. We cannot do it all and we hit the mother-wall and crash.

For the first few years of my children's lives, I only had portraits of them together. We never had family pictures taken and the reason was because I was too stressed to sit for a picture. By the time I had all the kids washed, dressed, and their hair combed there was no time for me to do my own hair and makeup. Then I basically had to wrap them in cellophane to keep them clean until we got to the photo studio, keep my daughter from pulling out her pigtails, break up the fight between them in the car, prop them up in clothes they did not like, and then try to make them smile. I was so stressed I was not fit to be in a picture. Family portraits make me crazy. Even to this day, when I mention it is family picture time my kids run in all directions.

When you add the second baby to the mix things get twice as hard. When my first child was born, I would spend my evenings sterilizing everything he touched. Every toy he played with and every pacifier he put in his mouth would all be washed in blazing hot water. By the time my daughter came along four years later I was not as crazy. I would do my best to wipe down her toys when necessary, and if her pacifier fell on the floor, I would wipe it in my jeans before I put it back in her mouth. Apparently, so I am told, this is why my son catches every flu and my daughter is never sick. Once again, it is the mother's fault.

My mother had ten children. I never appreciated what she went through until I had my own. I cannot imagine feeding, clothing, and trying to discipline ten children. I asked my mother one time why I did not have any baby pictures. To which she answered, "I was too busy cooking, cleaning and working to take pictures." Later she gave me a baby picture of one of my sisters. I told her, "That's not me," and she informed me, "No one is going to know the difference, just put it in a frame and say it's you." I told her, "I'm not doing that." She answered, "Why? That's what I did for your sisters. They all think that picture is of them." I do not even know if that picture is of any of us! It could be a neighbour's kid for all I know.

Whenever I asked my mother about raising children she would say, "If you never have them to make you laugh, then you'll never have them to make you cry, but you laugh a lot more than you cry."

I decided that as a mother there were three things I would do every day for my kids: 1. Tell them I love them and kiss and hug them no matter who is around or where we are; 2. Make them laugh out loud even if I had to hold them down and tickle them; 3. Make them feel good about themselves in some way. That is really all anyone can do besides providing the basic necessities of life.

Maya Angelou, the famous American poet, once said: You do the best you can and when you know better, you do better.

That has been my motto for twenty years. There is no book, there is no instruction manual, there's no one who can tell you how to do it. You just do the best you can and hope they do not grow up to write a book about you called "Mommy Dearest."

HUBBY ASKED, "WHY DO YOU LET CHRISTMAS STRESS YOU OUT?" SO, I KILLED HIM

Hubby is sitting in his comfortable chair, playing solitaire on his iPad, and watching the sports channel out of the corner of his eye.

I have just put together the upside-down Christmas tree – my fifth tree. I spent the afternoon wrapping gifts to give to extended family and friends. After two months of shopping, I have finally found the perfect gift for everyone. I do not believe in gift cards – it is too easy.

Sweat is dripping off my brow, turning my hair into a mass of unruly curls. I am wearing yoga pants and I have not been to yoga in weeks.

As hubby rocks back and forth in his chair my mind is racing like a derailed train...Did I forget anyone? I still have to go to the liquor store. I do not have any scotch tape. Did I put the towels in the dryer? Will we have roast or chicken for supper tomorrow night? Is homework done? Should I buy a turkey this week or wait till mid-December because the grocery store was out of stock a week before Christmas last year?

I cannot breathe. I feel like someone is pushing my head underwater and I am going down for the last time. I feel a pain in my chest and the sweat is stinging my eyes. Hubby is quietly playing solitaire. "Can you get me a bottle of water?" he asks.

Imagine the scene in the movie Carrie where they pour the bucket of blood over her head, igniting the devil in her to come forth and wreak havoc on the town. That is what I looked like. He looks up at me. "I'll get it myself," he whimpers.

"Why do you do this to yourself? Every year you stress yourself out over Christmas," he complains.

In my head I am holding my brass Nutcracker with both hands, swinging it like a baseball bat, bludgeoning him to death, while I am laughing and laughing and laughing. I know I have to be convicted by a jury of my peers, which will be twelve women drove to the brink of madness by Christmas stress.

Men just do not feel the stress of Christmas like women do.

Men buy for one person, their significant other.

Women have to buy gifts for in-laws, the outlaws, the music teacher, the dance instructor, the mailman, nephews, nieces, sisters, brothers, not to mention their own children and husbands!

They take the same budget that pays the mortgage, the utility bills, and the groceries, then stretch it even further to accommodate the two months of Christmas.

What is it about Christmas that makes women crazy? Why does this holiday make us want to turn our houses into showplaces that would rival the city of Paris at night? Set out tables that Martha Stewart would stand up and applaud. Bake cakes and cookies when we do not bake them at any other time during the year!

Red cherries, green cherries, do they taste the same? They do to me, but apparently there are women who can taste the difference. God forbid you make a cherry cake with green cherries because the grocery store is sold out of the red ones. NO ONE WILL EAT IT!!!

I notice hubby is no longer rocking. He is staring at me with his mouth open like a deer in the headlights. He does not know if I am going to pounce or wait until he is asleep and then strike.

I noticed I have not inhaled in about five minutes. I have just been staring at him with my eyes as big as saucers. Standing in front of my upside-down tree holding a pair of glittery balls in my hand. A bead of sweat falls from the tip of my nose. I finally suck air into my lungs. It sounds like I have come up for my last breath.

"Did you put the towels in the dryer?" I ask him. "Doing it now," he answers as he jumps to his feet. He carefully keeps his back to the wall and a safe three-foot radius between us as he walks toward the basement.

I look back at the upside-down tree and see my reflection in the big silver bulb. Carrie on prom night. Funny how I can combine Halloween and Christmas so easily. Martha Stewart would be proud. I continue to trim my tree, laughing on the inside because I know hubby will sleep with one eye open while I dream of sugar plums dancing in my head.

Ah, sugar plums. Is that a thing? How do you make sugar plums? I must remember to Google that. They might make a nice centrepiece. Is the cat in? Is the door locked? Is the stove off? Is Christmas over?

FEAR

"Only Thing We Have to Fear Is Fear Itself,"
Franklin D. Roosevelt

Humans are the only living creature that will sense fear but will not run from it.

God gave every living creature an internal mechanism that lets them sense fear and respond to save their lives. If you make a sudden move towards a dog or cat they will bolt from the room.

A personal safety expert on a TV show once said women are the worst when it comes to their personal safety. He explained through research he learned that if a woman were waiting for an elevator and the doors opened to expose a seedy-looking biker type guy with one hand behind his back like he was hiding something (like a knife) eight out of ten women would get on the elevator with him.

They would get in because they would not want to seem impolite or ignorant. The other two said they would have pretended they forgot something and walk away. None would say, "No thanks, I'll wait for the next elevator." Even though every fibre in their body, that God-given mechanism to sense fear, tells them not to get into the elevator, most would. They will put a stranger's feelings ahead of their own security.

Think about it: they would willingly walk into a steel box with a stranger that creeped them out, where no one could hear them scream, rather than make the guy feel bad about himself.

The expert explained the same experiment with men had different results. Five out of ten did not get into the elevator. Two said they would wait for the next elevator. Three got in because they knew they were bigger than the guy who was in the elevator but would be ready to defend themselves if anything happened.

Interesting stuff.

I am a big believer in going with your gut instinct or my "Spidy Senses." They have never failed me. I always thought I would be able to handle a situation where I felt fearful but, it turns out, I would not.

Recently I woke from a nightmare. I dreamed that I was lying in my bed half asleep (as I was). I was sleeping in, as I had worked a late shift. I could hear my son about to leave the house to catch the morning school bus. I heard another male voice talking to him, but I could not make out who it was. Then I heard my daughter's voice. She had caught the school bus a half hour earlier. I called out, "Who are you talking to?" My son yelled back, "Guess who is home from school sick." Then I thought, how did she get home? I could hear heavy footsteps coming up the stairs towards my bedroom and a man walked into my room. He said, "She was sick, and I brought her home." I was confused and said, "She's not allowed to leave the school with anyone but me."

Before I could finish the sentence, the man lay on the bed next to me and put his hand over my face. I was screaming, "Stop, Stop!" but the words would not come out. At that moment I woke up, shaking, not knowing if it was real or not. I ran downstairs, no one was around. I ran back upstairs and looked at the clock. It was 9:30 AM. Everyone was gone to school. It was just a weird dream. I went back downstairs and put coffee on and let the dog out in the back yard.

It was such a nice morning that I left the dog out and locked the back door while I jumped in the shower. I was shampooing my hair when I heard footsteps coming upstairs. I knew both doors were locked so I said to myself, "It's just your mind playing tricks on you. Don't go there." I continued to rinse the shampoo out and thought I heard someone walking from room to room. I thought if anyone were in the house the dog would be barking by now. Then it hit me. I locked the dog outside. I told myself, "Get a hold of yourself. You had a bad dream and now you are paranoid. Every woman thinks there is an axe murderer outside the shower curtain. Stop being so dramatic. What are you going to do? Fight him while you are naked?"

I continued showering when I thought I heard the toilet flush in the ensuite off my bedroom. I thought to myself, I should jump out and lock the bathroom door or open the window so if anyone were out there at least the neighbour would hear me scream. My gut and my Spidy Senses were screaming at me to sense the fear and protect myself, but the woman in me was saying, "No, I don't want to give in to the fear."

At that moment, the bathroom door opened, and my husband poked his head in to say he was home because he forgot something. I let out a blood-curdling scream and called him everything but a good Catholic. I shook for the rest of the day.

What really pissed me off about the whole thing was

that I know better. I know I should not have left the dog outside while I put myself in the most vulnerable position – in the shower, away from the phone. When I heard the first sound of someone in the house I should have jumped out, locked the door, put on a bathrobe, and called out the window to my neighbour, who I knew was in her yard gardening.

I should have looked for something in a drawer that I could have defended myself with. But I did not. I was afraid to look like I was crazy. That mistake could have cost me my life.

Then I thought of my daughter. What would she do if a stranger rang the doorbell and forced himself in? What would she do if she were home alone and heard someone downstairs?

I remember watching an interview with the father of a missing child. He said, "I taught my son to play baseball. I taught him to respect his elders, but I never taught him how to scream. Screaming would have saved his life. A stranger asked him to go for a walk and he was too polite to say no."

On the surveillance video you can see the stranger smiling at the boy and extending his hand. The boy is a little hesitant at first but reaches up and takes his hand. Then they walk away. Never to be seen again. The way he hesitated proves his gut told him not to go but he did not listen to it.

I taught my kids to scream. When they were toddlers, I always told them if someone makes you feel uncomfortable or tries to take you, scream "Fire." No one looks at a child crying, screaming "No." They may think it was a temper tantrum. Everybody comes running when you scream "Fire."

I thought I was the one woman who would look into the elevator and say, "I'll wait for the next one, thanks," but apparently, I am the woman who would walk right in.

We are given all kinds of warning signs before danger happens. Maybe my nightmare was my mind's way of saying: "Be on alert! Don't get into the elevator!"

Today I will sit down with my children and go through the "Stranger danger" rules again. Today I will teach my children that it is okay to be impolite if your gut tells you something is not right. Today I will make sure they remember how to scream.

Today I will give these same lessons to myself. God created "Women's Intuition" for a reason, it is that mechanism that protects us. Listen to it.

Do not be that woman who gets in the elevator. Be the woman who says, "No thanks. I'll wait for the next one."

Then do not apologize for it.

MADONNA'S REBEL HEART TOUR -- AND WHY I AM NEVER EATING FISH TACOS AGAIN

While Madonna and her flying nuns were pole dancing on crucifix stripper poles, I was throwing up on a security guard in the lobby of the Air Canada Centre, swearing to the EMS workers that I was not drunk!

I should start this story from the beginning….

Months and months ago I sat at my computer, continuously typing my seat preference into the Air Canada Centre's ticket screen to get Madonna tickets – the Holy Grail of all concert tickets. Her Rebel Heart Tour was crossing Canada and I was not going to miss it. I sat there for about twenty minutes pressing the button like I was playing a Swinging Bell machine. Then, finally, Jackpot! Two tickets to see Madonna live in concert in Toronto on October 5th!

Hubby and I talked about it for months. Counting down the weeks, then days, then hours till we were on a plane and on our way. The weekend was going to be perfect. We spent our first day at the outlet mall where I bought the most beautiful Michael Kors purse. Then we went to supper at the CN Tower 360 Restaurant. The next day we drove around Toronto, anxiously waiting for eight o'clock to go to the Air Canada Centre to see the Queen of Pop.

Around six o'clock we went to supper at a pub near the Air Canada Centre. I was too excited to eat so I just had a salad and fish tacos. At seven o'clock we got in the lineup waiting for the doors to open with all the other Material Girl fans and a homeless cat.

Seriously, the cat was homeless. It was sat on a pole with a sign that said he could not make his rent.

Finally, the doors opened and after buying over $100 in merchandise to shut me up, hubby and I went to our excellent seats!

Turns out Madonna is not a fan of being on time and did not start until 9:45. Luckily, there were enough drag queens and characters in the audience to keep me occupied. The last time I saw that many sets of prayer beads in the same room, I was at Catholic school and they certainly did not wear them with cone bras and lace tops. I was the only one in my row not wearing a sequin gown and I was most likely the only one born a girl.

Then the lights went down. The audience erupted. The drag queens cried, and I was on my feet. The most elaborate army of Chinese warriors carrying large crosses appeared on stage from thin air. A cage was lowered to the stage and "Like a Virgin" out she strutted.... Madonna in the flesh.

Everyone was in awe. The fourteen-year-old inside me wished I had also worn my cone bra and lace top. My stomach was flip-flopping with excitement.

The show was nothing short of phenomenal. You will never see another show like it.

An hour into the concert I realized my stomach was not flip-flopping with excitement, it was just flip-flopping, and I had to get to a bathroom quick. I looked at hubby and said, "I got to use the bathroom," and ran across four drag queens while Madonna sang "Like a Prayer."

This is when the night got interesting.

By the time I got to the bathroom I was sweating profusely and blacking out. Against all my mother's warnings, I sat on a public toilet seat without wiping it down first and then lost about five pounds.

The sweat was burning my eyes and I was screaming in my head, "Not now! Not now! I need to get back to Madonna!" I tried to stand up, but my legs were like rubber. I texted hubby and said, "Woman down in the bathroom, come quickly!"

A few moments later I heard him calling out my name. I managed to get myself together and stagger out of the bathroom. I could tell from the look on his face that I did not look like the Material Girl I once was.

The colour was drained from my face. Even my lips were white. My hair was soaking wet and I was dragging my coat behind me.

"Are you alright? You look like hell!" He grabbed me by the waist and dragged me to a side door. "You need some air." A security guard opened the door and put a chair outside so I could sit down.

"I think I just got overcome with heat. I am alright now," I told hubby and the security guard. I stood to walk back into the arena, then a sudden urge to die came over me and I ran back to the door, but the security guard was not as quick on his feet as hubby, who had moved out of the way, and while the Material Girl sang "Material Girl" I threw up all over my new fake snakeskin cowboy boots and the security guard.

I kept apologizing in between heaves and he kept saying it was okay, but I knew he secretly hated me.

EMS responders showed up and took my vitals while

asking me, then hubby, then me, then hubby, again and again how much I had to drink and what drugs I had been taking.

"Smell the vomit!" I told him. "I didn't have anything but fish tacos." But I knew from the look on their faces they did not believe me.

If I had known I was going to throw up on a security guard and pass out at a Madonna concert I would have drank a bottle of Vodka just to look cooler than I did at that moment, standing in a pile of puked up fish tacos!

After sizing up the mess and realizing I was completely sober, they cleaned me up and gave me some water. "More than likely food poisoning," one EMS said. I was determined to see the end of the concert, so hubby tried to get me back to our seats. I got to the top of the stairs and knew if I threw up on the drag queens, they would scratch my eyes out, and I was in no shape to take on a queen in five-inch heels and a micro mini. So, hubby dragged me back to the hotel room.

While I got cleaned up for bed hubby went to get me some water. By the time he got back I was passed out, naked on the bathroom floor with my arms around the toilet, and I woke up to him putting cold cloths on my forehead.

"Don't move me, don't move me," I protested, "I have to stay here tonight."

Hubby sat on the edge of the bed, waiting, and trying to figure out what to do next, while I lay on the floor hugging the toilet. Then I remembered something....

"Remember the romantic evening we had planned?" I asked him.

"You smell like puke. I think that ship has sailed." He smiled back.

"Actually, the look on your face right now looks strangely familiar and I just remembered where I've seen it before.... Our first date!"

"Really?" he raised an eyebrow.

"Our first date was a concert at the university. I was hosting the concert and I was extremely nervous about being on a first date and bringing a cop, who looked like a cop, to the Student Centre. So, I drank too much to make myself look cooler. Then we went back to your place and just when you were about to kiss me, I threw up, and you spent the night holding my hair out of the toilet and putting cold cloths on my forehead!"

I was surprised at the accuracy of my memory at that moment.

"This is romantic! It is a total recreation of our first date. Except I am throwing up fish tacos instead of beer and my hair is short, so you don't have to hold it out of the toilet."

"It was red," he answered dully

"What was red?"

"What you were throwing up on our first date. You were drinking coolers.... And they didn't make you any cooler."

"Oh, I can't believe you remembered, that's so sweet!"

He picked my limp body off the floor, helped me get into bed and wiped the dried puke off my face. Then, in a final act of true love, he moved my new Michael Kors purse to the other side of the room.

"Where are you going with that?" I asked.

"Moving it so you don't throw up in it."

"My God, that's the sweetest thing you've ever done for me."

I choked back a tear, then realize it was more fish tacos coming up and ran for the toilet.

We may have missed the end of the Madonna Rebel Heart concert, but my rebel heart was very content laying on the floor of a hotel bathroom watching hubby watch Sports Desk while I sang "Crazy for You" in between heaves of fish tacos.

HAPPY FATHER'S DAY MOM!

I bought my first Father's Day card when I was thirty-two years old. It was my son's first Father's Day.

Up until then I did not know the exact date for it. All I remember about Father's Day is it was that dreaded week in June when the fatherless kids were told to colour and keep quiet while the other kids spent what seemed like hours making Father's Day cards from construction paper.

My father left when I was five. That story would take more than a few pages in this chapter. It would need a whole book.

Let's just say that was the nicest thing he ever did for me.

My mother became both parents. She raised ten kids on her own and ran a boarding house on top of it. She cooked three hot meals for over twenty people every day, starched sheets, and could plaster and paint like a professional. She was the first woman to prove to me that women really could have it all, children, and a career!

I grew up in a politically incorrect world. Back then schoolbooks described the perfect, happy family as a mother, father, son, and daughter. If your family did not reflect that you felt like the poor cousin at the table. Every permission slip came home with a note to be signed by your father or mother, not your guardian.

I went to an all-female, Roman Catholic school taught by nuns or women who should have been nuns. I remember one class project. We had to draw a picture of our wedding day and how the church played a part in that day (I was in grade two). Each girl drew a picture of herself in a big fluffy white wedding gown. Some were standing at the altar, some were walking down the aisle, and some drew their family standing with the priest after the ceremony. I drew me (wearing my fluffy wedding dress) and my mother, hugging each other with big smiles on our faces.

Each of us took turns standing in front of our grade two classmates explaining our future self-portraits, and the teacher asked each girl questions about who was in the picture and what was happening.

Me, being painfully shy at that age, quickly ran up front and said, "This is me and my Mom on my wedding day," then ran back to my desk. The teacher called me back and asked, "Who else will be at your wedding?" I pondered, "I don't know."

She asked, "What about your father? He'll be giving you away."

"I don't have a father." Laughter broke out in the class.

"Everyone has a father. Your father gives you away at your wedding," she informed me at eight years old. "My mother will give me away," I told her.

"Mothers don't give you away. It has to be your father." I sat back in my desk thinking I would never get married at eight years old because I did not have a father. I never forgot her voice.

Truth was, very few kids I knew had both parents. I can only think of two families on my block that did.

The picture of the shiny, happy family on the cover of our Roman Catholic catechism did not exist on my block. I would imagine it did not exist on a lot of blocks.

These politically incorrect times were awkward at times.

Our school held an annual father-daughter banquet. I went one year with my mother. I think she was the only mother who attended. The other mothers were serving cold plates.

She was politely directed to the kitchen. She walked over to the nearest table, put her purse on the chair and said, "I'll sit here." I remember sitting at the long table filled with fathers and daughters, thinking that I wished we were not there. Looking back on it now, I wonder was it her way of sending me a message that I was just as good as everyone else and a small protest on her part to send a message to teachers that times were changing.

Nowadays single-parent families are the norm. Teachers are incredibly careful when they discuss what a family is. It is no longer just mother and father and kids. Sometimes it is just a mother, sometimes just a father, sometimes two mothers, and sometimes two fathers. The definition of family has changed... for the better.

The only thing that is important is a loving environment for kids. Everything else is secondary.

After my first child was born, I realized that being a mother is a damn hard job.

The first time I picked out a Father's Day card I bought two. One for my husband and one for my mother. Every year after that I gave my mother a Father's Day card. My thought being that if she was both mother and father to me then she deserved to celebrate both days.

This past week I was at a drug store looking for Father's Day cards. Just below "Happy Father's Day to My Brother" and just above "Happy Father's Day to Grand-Pa" was a new insert I had never seen before: "Happy Father's Day to My Mother." The slot was empty. They had sold out.

I guess I am not the only one who had both parents rolled into one.

HIDING EVIDENCE

I have hubby trained to call me when he is on the way home from work each day. Not because I really care if he has left work or not, or because I miss the sound of his voice when we are apart, but because I need time to hide the evidence.

What evidence?

ALL evidence! Evidence that may convict me in divorce court one day if he ever drags me there.

For example, the Tiffany Style Wisteria Table Lamp I ordered from the Home Shopping Channel. It was 60% off for two days only. I had to have it!

Up to five years ago I did not know what a Tiffany Style lamp was, then my sister showed me hers, and now I am obsessed with them. I have a dragonfly lamp, a butterfly lamp, a chicken lamp, an Aladdin Lamp, and now a Wisteria table lamp.

I have a deal with the mailman. If he sees my husband's truck, he cannot deliver any bag or box. He goes along with it too... I think he is afraid of me.

I put my new lamp on top of the piano and strategically placed dust and cat fur around it. This makes the lamp look like it has been there for years. Then I cut the box up and put it in the recycling bin and shred the bill. I chopped up the Styrofoam and buried it in the bottom of the garbage bucket and threw the contents of the kitchen garbage bucket on top of it.

It is all executed with the precision of a Navy Seal operation.

My ring from eBay came today. The mailman always delivers the mail before three o'clock, so the kids do not see anything either.

The ring is beautiful. It is big and gold-coloured with cubic zirconias all over it. I look like Joan Collins on the set of Dynasty when I wear it. It was only $10. I do not know where I will wear it. Maybe out walking the dog.

The box is already hidden in the recycling bin and the paperwork already shredded.

The mailman and I have worked out a system. He checks for hubby's truck. I watch for him from the kitchen window. We give each other the signal. If he has a box or parcel, he rings the bell twice to let me know there is a package in the mailbox. Why? Because the Postman always rings twice.

I get enough time to admire my latest acquisition and discard the evidence before hubby comes home.

If I get caught up admiring my latest adventure, hubby calls to warn me, or tell me, "I am on the way home." Sometimes he will say, "Why are you in such a rush to get rid of me? What are you up to?"

And I will brush him off and say, "Don't be so foolish."

As soon as I hang up the phone, I go into ninja mode. Chopping up boxes, shredding paper faster than a White House intern, hiding evidence.

For the record, the best place to hide evidence.... is in plain sight.

People always look under couches, in drawers, on top of closet shelves. No one ever sees what is in front of their face.

Then fifteen minutes later he comes through the door. "Something looks different. It is brighter in here. What did you do?"

"Oh, I moved the Wisteria lamp from the table in the basement and put it on the piano. I think it looks nicer there."

He stares at it for a few seconds. "It looks okay, I guess."

He hangs his coat in the closet then walks back toward me and my new lamp. "I never noticed it in the basement."

"It was on the table next to the bathroom," I lie.

Hubby is a retired police officer and hard to fool, but I am an expert at evidence tampering and he is no match for me.

"I must dust this piano off. The lamp already has cat hairs on it." He is still looking at me with that "What is she hiding?" look.

Evidence has blended in nicely.

Operation Wisteria complete.

GIRL'S NIGHT!

Dr. Phil, my TV BFF, says, "The most important person in a child's life is their same-sex parent." Whether you like Dr. Phil or hate him, you must agree that is true.

Mothers, or their female guardian, greatly influence their daughters.

I became very aware of this when my daughter was a toddler. She loved to sit and watch me put on my make-up. She would study every move I made and every object I touched. When I got up from my make-up dresser, she would sit down and put on her make-up, copying me move for move.

She loved going into my closet and taking out the highest pair of heels she could find. Then she would wear them around the house. Wobbling from room to room like she was walking on stilts. She would take down some glitzy dress I wore to a party, put it on and stand in front of the mirror. Sucking in her cheeks, shifting from hip to hip and practising her supermodel poses. Practising to be... me!

I am very conscious when I am getting dressed that she is watching everything from the length of my skirt to how much cleavage I am showing. She makes a mental note of it.

She is twelve now, going to junior high, and has become very self-conscious of how she looks. At twelve girls are trying to fit in. I would never want to be twelve again.

All her friends dress alike. If one gets a pair of red shoes, then everyone in the group must have red shoes. When I tell her, "I think those shorts are too short." She'll respond with, "What about those shorts you wore in Florida? They were short." Once again pulling out her mental notebook and reminding me that she is watching everything I do.

I try to explain that when a woman is in another country, where no one knows her, she can wear short shorts and a bikini if she stays out of the focus of a camera lens.

When she was about five, I started having "Girl's Night" when my husband took our son to cadets. As soon as they left, we would begin our beauty treatments. I buy those $1 facial kits at the drugstore. I do not really care if they "Deep clean" or if they're "Anti-aging." I go for the cool colours like purple or red or the flavoured ones like chocolate or strawberry.

During our girl's night we put our facials on, slice up some cucumber for our eyes and lay on my bed while talking about what is going on in her life. While waiting for our facials to work she has no trouble spilling all the secrets of her life: Who she likes. Who she doesn't. What she should do about it.

Then I give her a manicure and pedicure, telling her every step of the way how pretty and smart she is. We have a rule during our girl's night. Every hour we have to look in the mirror and say one thing we like about ourselves. Like "I like my hair," or "I am good at math."

Our girl's nights are not always spa nights. Sometimes

we go to a restaurant and talk or play a game. The whole purpose of our girl's night is to create an open line of communication with her, build her self-esteem and remind her about how special she is, not only to me, but to the world.

As she gets older, she wants to spend more time with her friends and less time with me. It is natural for that to happen, I keep telling myself.

She fits into my high heels now perfectly. We are the same size, but she still wobbles. I am sure in no time she will have the art of walking in three-inch heels perfected.

My Mother always warned me, "You don't own your children. You only have a loan of them. Eventually they grow up and leave you." That day seems to be coming toward me like a freight train. I cannot even think about the day she starts packing up her stuff to move. I cannot imagine when our girl's night stops.

She still will not go to sleep until I kiss her good night, and when she sleeps, she looks like a toddler. Letting go is not going to be easy for me.

As a mother, it is our job to teach our kids how to be independent. Fly the nest. Survive on their own. Leave us. It seems like we spend the first few years of their lives wishing they would grow up and go away. Then as the day gets closer, we wonder where the time went.

I have a few years of girl's nights left. She is only twelve. She still has some growing to do. But I realize she will always see herself in me. The career she picks, how she lets a man treat her, the way she dresses, will all be influenced by me.

That is why I've never been a "Do as I say, not what I do" kind of mom. I try to be the woman that I would like her to grow up to be. I pray she even does better than that.

I see my daughter as an extension of myself. The person who I would like to be. The friend I cannot wait to have. The overwhelming pride in my heart.

When she was about four, she gave me a Valentine's Day card. (I know my husband picked it out for her.) I keep the card tucked into the mirror on my make-up dresser to remind me that I am being watched, even when she is not in the room.

The poem on the front says:

I'm Mommy's "little shadow,"
going everywhere you go,
Dressing up to look like you,
because I love you so,
Yes, I'm walking in your footsteps
(or at least I'm trying to!)
'Cause I've got
my heart set, Mommy,
on being just like you!

HOW OFTEN CAN A WOMAN PEE?

My son has size ten feet, and he has not stopped growing yet. I knew when he was an embryo that he was going to have big feet because he used them to tap dance on my bladder for nine months. Four years later, his sister followed in his footsteps and spent the last six months locked in my womb kicking my bladder for fun.

As a result, I now have the ability to fill the Grand Canyon after drinking one bottle of water! While some women could read a magazine waiting for the flow to stop, I could read War & Peace.

Welcome to menopause! On top of night sweats and hot flashes, I now leak when I sneeze.

From research, I found out that light bladder leakage affects about forty million women. That means you can expect a third of your friends to know what you are going through.

I have often drove from St. John's to Gander and had to pull over on the side of the Trans-Canada Highway to run off in the woods to pee! I have this terrible fear that I am going to be squat down 100 feet from the pavement relieving myself when I look up and find a dead body. Then I would have to call the police to report what I found. Their first question will be, "What are you doing in this area?" "Oh officer, I was relieving myself." Not a chance, I would confess to the murder first.

A friend of mine is a police officer. She told me one cold winter's night she responded to an accident on the highway in the middle of nowhere. Five of her male counterparts showed up to help. She was the only female. They spent hours on the road clearing the scene. Then the urge to pee hit with a vengeance. While her male counterparts could turn their backs to the road and write their names in the snow, she would have to find a discrete location to squat down before her bladder burst. Every time she tried to sneak away someone would ask, "Where are you going?"

While standing in the cold night taking a statement from a male driver the urge to pee took over. She could feel a small stream beginning to leak down her leg until she could no longer hold it in and the dam broke. To say she "filled her boots" was an understatement. She thought that her police parka would hide the deed. That was until the hot pee hit the cold night and steam began to rise from her pants!

Another friend told me that she was on a ski trip to Marble Mountain when her bladder took her to new heights. She had taken the lift to the top of OMJ, one of the highest slopes, when the urge to pee became unbearable. She looked around for a facility but could not find one. She said there was no way she could ski to the bottom of the mountain while trying to hold her pee, so she decided to squat down behind a bush. She laid her ski poles down to the side and pulled her pants down around her knees.

Hearing other skiers fly by her, she quickly relieved herself and tried to shimmy her ski pants back up. What she did not account for was how slippery her skis were.

While trying to pull her pants up she began to slide. She grabbed for the ski poles but could not reach them and the movement only propelled her more. Before she knew it, she had skied out of the bush and onto the ski track. With her pants still around her knees and in her squat down peeing position, she was now barrelling down OMJ to the laughter of her fellow skiers.

The squat down position made her go faster, and without ski poles and unable to change leg positions because of her ski pants, she could not stop herself. Rather than end up at the bottom of the mountain with her pants around her knees, she decided to throw herself. When she did, one ski flipped over the other and she dislocated her knee. Now dying of embarrassment and in extreme pain she tried to pull her pants up, but people quickly formed a circle around her trying to help. Within minutes the First Aid team were on the slope with a Skidoo and got her off the mountain and transported to the hospital. On the plane back to St. John's, the passenger next to her pointed at her leg in a brace and asked, "Skiing accident?" "Yes," she replied. Then he added, "Did you hear about the girl skiing down OMJ with her pants around her knees?" "No!" she answered and put her headphones on, keeping her peeing – I mean skiing – accident to herself.

One night, while dining out with my husband, the urge hit me like a tractor trailer, and I dashed off to the ladies room. The waitress told me the bathrooms were located at the top of the stairs to the right. By the time I found it in the dimly lit hallway there was only one stall and lucky for me it was empty. Of course, bathroom stalls are only big enough for the stick figures on the door. It is a lesson in gymnastics to hoist a dress and tear down the control top pantyhose while trying not to spill a drop.

Then someone else came in and within seconds I could hear them urinating. I thought, "They're not using the sink, are they?" I finished and pulled up my control top pantyhose. Exiting the stall, I locked eyes with a man peeing in a urinal on the wall. Horrified, I said, "This is the ladies room!" and stomped out. I got back to my table and told my husband. He pointed out, "He was using the urinal? You were in the men's room!" Luckily, we were finished eating and my husband had paid the bill so I could run out without seeing this poor man again.

In addition to menopause, one in three of us can now expect a visit from the Poise Fairy, every time we sneeze.

If it is such a common thing, why hasn't the world adapted to us?

Why don't the change rooms in ladies' stores have a bathroom located in the same area?

How come every time I go to a concert there is a huge line up to the ladies room but no line up to the men's room?

We need more stalls!

I now must stop and cross my legs to sneeze. I have to stay dehydrated if I want to go shopping and try things on.

I thought when the babies were born, I would not have to worry about my water breaking again.

Apparently not. Menopause literally has me peed off!

I AM GOING TO STEP ON YOUR HUMBUG

Shopper's Drug Mart stopped playing Christmas music because customers complained it was too early.

Really?

Didn't they care about the customers who loved it?

I play Christmas music all year 'round. I have, I guess what would be considered an antique stereo system. It has a turntable. It also holds five CDs. It has held the same five CDs for a few years now: David Foster – The Christmas Album; Josh Groban – Noel; Andrea Bocelli – My Christmas; Country Christmas featuring various country artists; and, of course, Elvis Presley – Christmas Duets.

When I turn the stereo on it automatically goes to the CD player. In July, when I start cleaning the house on a Saturday morning the first thing I do is turn on the stereo for background music and it is instantly Christmas! All my angels are heard on high.

I am vacuuming to Elvis's "Blue Christmas", dusting to Andrea Bocelli's "Jingle Bells" and folding laundry to Josh Groban's "Silent Night". How can you get sick of Christmas music? What kind of cold-hearted, sick person are you?

You are supposed to have your Christmas spirit all year round. When I hear people say, "Oh no, Walmart has Christmas decorations out!" or "The neighbours have the tree up already!" I just want to kick them right in the jingle balls.

My tree goes up after Remembrance Day in November. I love putting the tree up. Every ornament on our tree has a special meaning: Our First Christmas together bulb, Baby's First Christmas silver boots, Baby Girl's First Christmas pink rattle. Everywhere we travel, we find a Christmas ornament to hang on our tree. I have a gold-plated Graceland ornament, Grand Ole Opry bulb, even a piranha wearing a Christmas hat from Roatan in Honduras! The tree is full to the brim with twenty years of memories.

Putting up the tree is not about getting an early start on Christmas for me. It is about re-living Christmases past. I do not have three ghosts to show me how my life could have turned out. I have a tree full of ghosts telling me how lucky I am.

The kids love decorating the tree with me. They get so excited going through the box of ornaments, finding the ones they picked out over the years and the ones about their lives. My son is finishing high school this year and plans to go to the Air Force to be a pilot. He will be moving to Kingston to start his engineering degree in September. Which means this will probably be the last Christmas that he will decorate the tree with me. I had a hard time holding back the tears when he found all his Star Wars ornaments and lined them up together on the tree like he has done since he was a little boy.

What is wrong with people? Don't we need a little Christmas all year long? I love Christmas. I love the parties, the decorating, the lights, the chocolate coconut-balls that everybody buys at Costco and pretends they made from scratch.

I love hiding the presents, wrapping the presents, opening the presents. I love going to Church to see the Christmas pageant, especially when the kids were in it.

I love a "White Christmas". I love dancing to "Rockin' Around the Christmas Tree" and I really love it when I am the "Mommy Kissing Santa Claus". How is it possible to hate Christmas music? Don't you feel the tears swell when Bob Seger sings "Little Drummer Boy"? Doesn't your heart swell when you hear John Lennon's "Happy Xmas (War is Over)"?

I remember being a high school cheerleader and dancing to "Jingle Bell Rock" from the Confederation Building to the Avalon Mall, wearing three pairs of nylons to stay warm.

Who does not do the actions to Madonna's "Santa Baby"? I always laugh when my BFF hears "Feliz Navidad" and changes the words to "Please marry Dot." It never gets old.

How do you not sing out loud to "Frosty the Snowman"? The words are tattooed on your brain for God's sake. And like you do not imitate Alvin during "The Chipmunk Song".

What about driving in the van singing, "Rudolph the Red Nosed Reindeer had a very shiny nose," and the kids in the back singing out, "Like a light bulb!"

Like you are not marching around the store when Snoopy's Christmas comes on.

Hubby loves Jim Reeves' "An Old Christmas Card". He sings it whenever it comes on and I love it when he does. I have kept every Christmas card he ever gave me because of that song.

I love Christmas music all year round because it brings

back such happy memories for me. Every song makes me smile, laugh, dance or cry. Even the VOCM Christmas song makes me cry.

I do not like people who don't like Christmas music.

Eight-year-old Virginia O'Hanlon wrote a letter to the editor of New York's Sun in September 1897.

She wrote:

DEAR EDITOR: I am 8 years old. Some of my little friends say there is no Santa Claus. Papa says, 'If you see it in THE SUN it's so.' Please tell me the truth; is there a Santa Claus?

The Editor of the Sun published his much-loved letter. Ending it with *"No Santa Claus! Thank God! He lives, and he lives forever. A thousand years from now, Virginia, nay, ten times ten thousand years from now, he will continue to make glad the heart of childhood."*

Humbug to you people who say Christmas comes too early each year. It should be Christmas all year round. Turn up the music, Shopper's Drug Mart. I will dance in your aisles.

I'VE GOT IT IN THE BAG

I do have it in the bag! My chiropractor tells me every week.

At each visit he lifts my purse and weighs it. He once clocked it at nine pounds.

It seems my purse and my butt have something in common, they are both getting bigger with age!

I have this weird attraction to big purses. The bigger the better. My purse is one size smaller than an airplane carry-on and one size bigger than a grocery bag.

My doctor told me to get rid of the big bags and downsize... and I did. I took everything out of my big bag and switch to a compact model. At my next visit, the doctor noted the smaller purse then lifted it. "It still weighs as much as a small child!" he scolded me.

"It's smaller," I protested. "But you didn't lose any of the content! You don't need all the stuff in here!" he informed me.

That night, I emptied the contents on top of my bed. My wallet weighs the most. I decided to start there. Tucked in one side – fifteen pictures of my kids. Starting with my son's kindergarten picture (he graduated from high school five years ago). Then various Walmart Christmas poses of the kids together, me and hubby, hubby and kids, me and kids, etc.

It dawned on me; I need to buy a photo album.

They all must go. Except the latest pictures of the kids and the picture of me and hubby wearing cowboy hats, and the one of daughter wearing the angel wings and son's kindergarten picture. All the rest are going in a photo album.

On the other side of the wallet are receipts. Receipts from Walmart, Canadian Tire, Sobeys, Lawton's, etc. Apparently, I shop a lot. The latest bill was from yesterday. I need to keep that just in case I need to return that $7 T-shirt to Walmart. The oldest one was from 2010. A toaster I bought at Canadian Tire. I wonder if they will take it back? I do have the bill after all!

I threw out a wad of bills that could choke a horse. Including the one for the $7 T-shirt from Walmart. If it falls apart, I am just going to have to suck it up.

On the outside of the wallet is the zipper compartment that is swollen like a fat lip. I pour out the change and count $13.75. Lots of pennies. Am I the only one still using pennies? I blame most of my back problems on the Canadian Mint. Carrying around these loonies and toonies is hard work. I need to keep the change for coffee and parking meters. I put the pennies in my daughter's piggy bank.

Behind the zipper is a long slot for paper money. There is none there. Who carries money anymore? It is just an ATM card and credit card. I need to keep both.

Now my wallet is about three pounds lighter.

On to the make-up bag.

It is full of blush, concealer, mascara, powder and four different colour lipsticks. It just occurred to me, it is the first time I've opened this make-up bag in about a year!

I never use this make-up. I put it on in the morning in my bedroom and do not touch it again till later in the day. (I keep the necessities – lipstick and face power – in a desk drawer at work.) I never use this make-up bag, but I cannot let it go.

The purse seems lop-sided without it. I may need it someday. I know if I take it out tonight, I will go looking for it tomorrow. I may need to do a total make-over while waiting at a red light. I decide to take out three lipsticks, but the bag stays.

At the bottom of the purse is an endless mess of tissues, Tic-Tacs, nail files, more receipts, more pennies, two more lipsticks. How did I become "The Old bag Lady?"

My mother once found a hammer and screwdriver in hers.

I once found the TV remote in my purse. It had been missing for about a week. We searched every chair cushion, nook and cranny in the house, but could not find it. I was at the check-out at the grocery store when I reached in to grab my wallet and pulled out the remote.

The truth is, you do not know what you're going to find in my purse when you put your hand in. I could be stranded on a desert island for months and survive on what is in my purse. It would be based on a strict diet of Tic-Tacs and Life Savers. My make-up would be perfect, but hubby would be pissed that he finally got months of uninterrupted TV but could not change the channels.

I downsized to a "lighter" model. I cannot give up the big purses; size does matter to a woman, too. But I lost about five pounds in the process. I cannot wait to visit my doctor to see what he has to say about my sudden weight-loss. My back does feel better.

It is like the weight of the girl has been taken off my shoulders!

I BROKE MY VAGINA IN SPIN CLASS. NO, IT'S NOTHING LIKE RIDING A BIKE!

My daughter talked me into doing a spin class with her. I have never done one before, but I imagined it was like riding a bike. How hard could it be?

First, you put on these special bike shoes that kind of feel like small ski boots when you walk in them. Then you get on the stationary bike and the shoes lock into the pedals. The instructor said it was to keep your feet from falling off, but I realized halfway through class, it is really to keep you from running away.

The class started and the instructor turned the hip hop music up to ten and turned off all the lights. The place was pitch black except for two lit candles on the instructor's raised stage. It kind of looked like a Satanic worship studio.

Then she started yelling out instructions through an attached microphone and the class began peddling. She quickly began to speed up and I could not hear a thing she was saying over the Devil Worship music, so I just mimicked everyone around me. I figured I would do what everyone else was doing. I did not hear her say, "Go at your own pace."

Determined to prove that I was in great shape, I tried to keep up with the twenty-something girl in front of me who was peddling so fast it looked like her arse was chewing bubble gum.

Then the instructor shouted, "Push, push, push!" Which felt appropriate because the last time my Vajayjay felt this sore I was trying to push a head the size of a watermelon out of a hole the size of a Cheerio.

She yelled, "Stand up and get to the top of this hill!"

Which was the best part of the class because I forgot how hellishly hard a bicycle seat is. After five minutes I began to feel chafing where there should never be any chafing.

Two minutes later she yelled for us to sit back down. I discretely tried to adjust myself on the seat without feeling like I was getting kicked in the Vajayjay. I took the hand towel hanging from the front of the bike, folded it, and put it on my seat. It lasted until she screamed for us to stand and my towel hit the floor.

Remember, I am locked on this bike and I cannot bend over and pick up the towel. Now I have no way to wipe away the sweat that is burring my eyes.

I am burning at both ends. Literally!

I notice the class is standing and sitting repeatedly while pumping their arms on the handlebars. I cannot hear what the instructor is saying but I am determined to keep up. It becomes a ten-minute punishment of – ride up hill – get sexually assaulted by a bicycle seat - ride up hill – get sexually assaulted by a bicycle seat - ride up hill – get sexually assaulted by a bicycle seat.

Oh, and pump your arms like you love it.

I look around at the rest of the class and realize I am the only one here who was born in the 60s. I really start to question my own judgment.

When I told my daughter I wanted to spend some time

with her I was thinking of going to lunch not re-enacting the twelve hours of labour it took to bring her into this world.

After forty-five gruelling minutes it finally stopped. The instructor turned the lights back on and the music off. I forgot my feet were locked into the pedals and I jumped off the bike, landing hard on the cross bar. Luckily, my face was already soaking wet from the sweat so no one could see my tears.

When I got off the bike my legs were shaking so bad, I felt like I was walking on the moon. I took off the shoes and painfully walked to the bathroom. Just when I thought the worst was over, I sat on the toilet and tried to pee.

I can only describe it as acid being poured over my chafed privates.

I stopped the urine midstream and held it in… for four days! At one point I begged my daughter to take me to the hospital so I could get a catheter.

A full tube of Polysporin and an ice pack later, I could finally let a little pee out.

Not enough to pass a drug test. But just enough so my bladder did not burst.

I found out after class that there are biking shorts with a padded seat (would have been nice to know) and eventually your Vajayjay "gets used to it." That is never going to happen for me.

The next time I want to have mother-daughter time, I will be picking the activity.

I hope she enjoys a good old-fashioned enema!

WHO HASN'T THROWN THEIR BACK OUT TAKING OFF CONTROL TOP PANTYHOSE AND SPANX?

I have. I am not even joking. Here is what happened....

Friday night hubby BBQed ribs and, as usual, cooked way too many, but they were cooked to perfection with smoked hickory sauce dripping from their crispy grizzle. (I know I look at food the same way some women look at men).

Then Saturday afternoon I cooked a big brunch with bacon, sausage, eggs, hash-browns, and toast. That night we had friends over for supper. Hubby went back to the BBQ with big, juicy prime-rib steaks and I made German potatoes (these are cooked with a full pack of bacon, then the onions are sautéed in the bacon fat and poured over the potatoes). I topped it off with my famous broccoli casserole.

Well, Sunday is family supper night and we had baked chicken with all the fixings. Needless to say, come Monday morning I was not fitting comfortably in my skirt.

I tried putting a wire hanger through the eye of the zipper pull. While I pulled down on the skirt with one hand and pulled up with hanger in the other hand, the hook on the hanger gave way and straightened out under the strain, and I ended up punching myself in the face.

I laid across the bed and tried to pull the button closer to the hole, but there was a better chance of getting Heather Mills & Paul McCartney back together before this button and the hole.

I finally gave in and decided to take out the big guns... Spanx and control top pantyhose.

Putting Spanx on is an art form. You must carefully shimmy them up past your knees and hips. Then when you get the fork in place you carefully roll them up over your hips and stomach like you are rolling up a jellyroll. You take your final deepest breath, then roll them past your rib cage until they rest comfortably under your breasts. Be careful not to accidentally tuck a nipple in because you will pay for that when you stand up.

Once the Spanx are safely in place, I start on the control top pantyhose. Carefully unrolling them up over my ankles, then knees, taking them to the breaking point of their stretch capabilities over the hips and stomach, then twisting them till they fall in place.

It is the "Latest celebrity diet!" Twenty minutes to put on Spank and pantyhose, four inches disappear off my waist and three off my thighs. I make a mental note to remember to check the Weight Watchers Guide to see if putting on Spanx and control top pantyhose is in their exercise section. I should get at least ten points for that.

Once everything is in place, my skirt slips on without a problem. It is a little baggy now around the stomach. I am pleased with my accomplishment.

Everything was great until I came home from work. As usual, I am in a rush to get my daughter to her music class. I run upstairs to take off my suit and begin the decompression process. I carefully roll the control top pantyhose over my stomach, past my hips and down to my knees.

I gain three inches back. I sit down on the bench in my room.

I roll the Spanx over my stomach, to my hips. Lunch begins to digest, and I gain the last three inches back. It was like opening a big bag of pink home insulation. The entire mid-section of my body starts to expand and loosen.

I stand up and bend to roll the pantyhose past my knees. I feel the most God-awful pain starting in my lower back and running through the left side of my body. I am sure I have been shot.

I land on the floor, curled up in a ball with shocks of pain going through my body, and let out a blood curdling scream.

My daughter comes running into the room.

"What happened?"

"I don't know." I think I am having a heart attack, but I do not want to scare her. "Call your father and tell him to get home now."

"I should call an ambulance!" she screams. At first, I think, yes that is a good idea. Then I look down and notice my knees are still tied together with the control top pantyhose and the Spanx are constricting my hips and blood flow. I have visions of a paramedic writing something about "Fifty Shades of Grey" in his report on me.

"NO!" I scream. "No ambulance!" She helps me finish taking the pantyhose off. Then she helps me up from the floor and acts as a crutch as I limp towards the bed, moaning in pain with each step. I roll onto the mattress.

I knew my next request would ensure her need for counselling someday but by then she would be married and not my problem.

"I need you to get me some normal underwear and help me get the Spanx off." The look on her face was sheer terror, but I was determined that if the good Lord was going to take me, it would be in comfortable underwear. If this was to be my daughter's last memory of me, then so be it. It is not like I asked her to change my bedpan.

With her eyes clenched shut, she tugged at the Spanx until they came off, threw the comfortable underwear at me, and ran out of the room.

By the time hubby arrived I was curled up in a ball on the bed, in wracks of pain.

I refused to go to the hospital until the indents from the Spanx had disappeared from around by body.

Four hours later the doctor at the Emergency Room confirmed I had a pinched nerve in by back.

Five days later, with the help of a bottle of muscle relaxers and pain killers, I could finally walk upright. I only felt a slight pull in my left hip when I sat or stood quickly.

Tonight, Hubby is taking me to supper and a show with friends. I have to fit into a dress. I have spent the entire week on the couch, unable to move, eating Halloween chips. I walk into my closet; the dress hangs on one side; the Spanx and control top pantyhose are on a shelf on the opposite side. It is like the showdown at the O.K. Corral.

What have I learned? I am a slave to my vanity.

I begin the arduous process of pulling the Spanx up over my knees, shimmying them past my hips and stomach, taking that final breath as I roll them past my rib cage. Instantly I lose three inches.

I catch a glimpse of myself in the mirror. I look like a Polish sausage but nothing jiggles. Yay me!

BOY BANDS: ROLLERMANIA FOREVER! THE TARTAN ARMY LIVES ON

I loved Les! Which Bay City Roller did you love? Remember Rollermania?

Bang! Bang! Bang! My bedroom door bends in the middle from my mother's fist pounding it from the other side.

"Turn the music down for Jesus sakes, I can't hear myself think!"

Inside the room Rollermania had hit hard. My friends and I were listening to the latest Bay City Rollers record on my hi-fi (which is nothing like Wi-fi). Jumping up and down till the floorboards were reaching their maximum capacity. Screaming to the top of our lungs "S.A.T.U.R.D.AY. Night", "Keep on Dancing" and "Bye Bye Baby." I loved Les with his dark brown curly hair and his Scottish accent! Karen loved Woody with his long straight blond hair. They were so handsome and Scottish, too. That accent drove us into a frenzy.

They were the "Tartan teen sensations from Edinburgh" and the biggest thing since The Beatles. Long before Justin Bieber and One Direction, there were the Bay City Rollers: worldwide teen idols and one of the most screamed-at teeny-bopper acts of the 1970s.

My room was wallpapered with their pictures, torn from Teen Beat magazine and anything else we could get our hands on. There was no internet or "Fan Pages" back then. Just an address in Scotland to write to if you wanted to join their "Official Fan Club" and I did. We all did.

We longed to hear the announcers at CJON tell us the Bay City Rollers were going to play at our hometown stadium. We would have lined up for days, weeks, or months to get a ticket.

We were devoted Rollers fans. My Mother lost her mind when she found out I cut up my new jeans, made them four inches shorter and sewed tartan to the cuffs and down the sides of the legs.

She nearly had a stroke when I came out of the bathroom after cutting my hair like Eric's. A handful of Dippity-do making it spikey on top and a half a can of Final Net keeping the sides straight and feathered.

Then she came home from Woolworths with a blue Bay City Rollers T-shirt. It had their five faces on the front and tartan on the sleeves. I cried. I could not believe you could buy a Rollers T-shirt in St. John's. I wore it every day. I wore it under the white shirt I had to wear with my blue school tunic. I rolled the tartan sleeves up so Sister would not see it. But she did and told me never to wear it again with my uniform or it would become the property of the Sisters of Mercy!

The Bay City Rollers had sold an estimated seventy million records. Then in 1976 Alan Longmuir left the group. It was the beginning of the end for Rollermania. We were heartbroken. I was twelve years old and refused to believe that Les did not love me as much as I loved him. It felt like he had personally broken up with me.

By that time Paul McCartney was charting with Wings' "Silly Love Songs", Wild Cherry was telling us to "Play That Funky Music", and Disco was on the horizon. My Bay City Rollers posters were replaced with Saturday Night Fever posters, pictures of Peter Frampton and the Bee Gees.

There was no internet so I could not find out what became of Les or the rest of the Rollers. Then a few weeks ago, my daughter asked for a record player!

I know right! A record player for her bedroom. I did not think they existed anymore but apparently, they are making a comeback. "Where can you buy records?" I asked her. "Everywhere," she tells me. Records are making a comeback, too.

I used to have thousands in my basement. A few years ago, stretched for storage space, hubby talked me into giving them away. Some guy with a pickup truck and a few friends came and emptied my basement of all my teenaged memories. I did keep a few though: Michael Jackson's Thriller, a few Elvis (of course), Meatloaf's Bat Out of Hell, Bruce Springsteen's Born in the USA, and of course, the Bay City Rollers.

I put the Rollers' album on her new record player, and they sounded just as good. The first note of "Saturday Night" sent me back to when I was a ten-year-old girl bouncing in my bedroom with my girlfriends, screaming to the top of our lungs. Planning our weddings to the Bay City Rollers.

I had to Google them. The Tartan Army still exists! Les McKeown, the lead singer, is touring under the name "Bay City Rollers." He looks a little different now... but so do I. He has dates set for 2015 all around the UK.

I got a little flushed... this complete stranger from Edinburgh who, at ten, I swore to love till I died, was still touring. I am a little giddy.

Anyone want to go? Can you imagine being in the audience?

I know you would not jump to your feet and turn into a ten-year-old girl when he sang "Saturday Night." Come on, let's go!

Love you Les!!!!

IS IT WRONG TO PLAN A MAN'S MURDER WHEN HE IS SICK, EVEN IF IT IS ONLY IN YOUR HEAD?

I have spent many a night rocking a sick child with a fever so high their little head would leave scorch marks on my cheek.

I cannot tell you how many times I had spit-up down my back or puke over my front and it doesn't bother me in the least.

If my kids are sick, I am there. Wiping the puke, changing the sheets, measuring the Advil, never once losing my temper. It does not bother me one bit.

But as soon as my husband says he has a cold, I want to put the pillow over his face.

I do not know why this happens to me! I am not a violent person, but as soon as he sneezes, I want to punch him in the head.

Maybe it is because he wakes me up to tell me he's sick ten times a night. Maybe it is because he flops around the bed moaning and groaning like he's dying of a near fatal disease.

Or maybe it is because he follows me around the house telling me how sick he is and leaving his snotty tissues on the coffee table for me to pick up.

Why do men think they married their mothers?

My husband followed me around the house with a

pair of pants hanging over his arm, telling me he needed a button sewn on. I was making lunches for the next day, trying to negotiate a truce with my pre-teen daughter on what she was going to wear to school, while pushing my teenaged son to get in the shower, feed the dog, and check homework.

"Do I look like your mother? Do I look like I own a sewing basket?" If pants need a button, throw them out and buy a new pair!

Then he plays the hide and seek game with me. "Where's my tie clip?" How the hell do I know? When was the last time I wore his tie clip? "You're always hiding stuff on me!" he says. "If you'd only put stuff back where it belongs! It's not hiding, it's cleaning up!" Like I have time to hide his tie clip.

I did hide the tie clip that time just to mess with his mind.

"I don't remember you graduating from the School for the Deaf," I tell him all the time. No matter what I say he will say "What?" I know he hears me because if I do not answer he'll repeat what I said and answer me.

This man can stand on our back patio, watch a golf game on our TV through the living room window (yes, he has it set up perfectly), and read the lips of the players, but he cannot hear me talking when I am standing right in front of him.

I know why women outlive men. Because men cannot live on their own.

If I died first, my husband would sit in his lounge chair watching golf forever. He would not know where his underwear or tie clip were because I'd take them in the casket with me just to piss him off!

He would never know what's for supper, or where the

children were. They would find him years from now, a skeleton in a lounge chair covered in cobwebs with a remote in his hand.

I know it is flu season. My kids are passing it back and forth.

It is like they lick each other to spread the germs. When kids are sick, they want Mom. No one wants to puke over Dad.

He stands in the hall asking, "Do you need any help?"

That is okay. I can handle it.

But when I am holding a kid's head over the toilet and a cold facecloth to their head, the last thing I want to hear is, "I feel so sick. I am going back to bed."

When I am sitting in that chair, rocking a sick child back to sleep and I hear snoring coming from the master bedroom, that is when I want to sneak in and just so lightly push the pillow over his head.

IN THESE SHOES!

I know exactly when my shoe obsession began. I was in grade two. It was the 70s.

Back then everybody wore "gators" or "galoshes" in the wintertime. They only came in black. I am sure you remember them. You put your shoe on first and then you put your shoe down in your gators and you fastened them with a little silver buckle that was on the side.

One day, a classmate showed up in red gators. They were like the Holy Grail of gators.

I became obsessed with them. I wanted red gators more than anything in the world, but she said her mother bought them on the mainland and they were not available in Newfoundland.

Every morning I would stare at those red gators in the coat room. It started my obsession with red shoes.

Now I cannot pass a shoe store if there are red shoes in the window. I must have them.

I love shoes. Who doesn't? The higher the better. The more ridiculous the better. They are like artwork to me. Nothing makes you feel more powerful than a three-inch black stiletto on a Monday morning. That means business!

I started having back problems in 2002 after having an

accident and it got progressively worse over the years. But it never stopped me from wearing my high heels. Even though my chiropractor would constantly tell me, "The heels are not helping." I would tell him, "I have a Barbie foot. I need high heels. If I wear a flat my back would go out." He never believed me. As I hobbled in his office I would say, "Just because you're in pain doesn't mean you have to be ugly." I will always wear my high heels.

On March 19, 2012, I had back surgery. I had two titanium rods attached to my lower spine to fix the damage and stop the pain. The day before I went into surgery, I went to a shoe store like a drunk getting his last drink before an AA meeting. I bought a pair of three-inch purple velvet shoes, even though I knew it would be a long time before I could wear them.

They were an incentive for me to get out of the bed and start walking again. My goal was to put them on September 1st, almost six months after my surgery, and wear them to work.

Bette Midler has a song called "In these shoes." It became my theme song for the next six months as I learned to live with this titanium spine. I am sure a lot of people would look at my situation and think that's a pretty silly thing to concentrate on as you recover.

I do not care. It is my thing.

I think shoes are to women what penises are to men. It is only three inches, but it makes us powerful beyond belief!

IT'S A HAIRY SITUATION

If I ever end up in a home for the bewildered, I have a pact with my daughter to pluck my chin hairs.

My greatest fear about growing old is not ending up in a home or having to wear Depends. It is that my eyes will get so bad I will not notice my chin hairs are reaching my nipples. (Which will be dragging on the floor by then anyway!)

I know beauty is on the inside, yadda, yadda, yadda, but I cannot handle the facial hair thing.

Along with everything else menopause brings, you can add excessive facial hair to the list.

This proves God is a man! Because if God were female, when women reached menopause their stomachs would get flatter, their breasts would get firmer, they would remember why they went upstairs, and would only have to pee once per day.

It has become an all-out war between me and my hormones.

I wake up in the morning, turn on my magnifying makeup mirror and began the daily hunt-and-peck. I feel like an adolescent boy searching for those first signs of becoming a man, except I am not a man. I am a middle-aged woman going through menopause and giving Mother

Nature the middle finger on a daily basis. I run my fingers under my chin, I can feel one, but I just cannot find it. At least they are now coming in white, so I do not notice them right away. A new trick I learned is to run my mascara lightly over the area, then they are easy to find.

It is so unfair. Hair on a man's body denotes strength and sexiness. Hair on a woman's body denotes old hag. While I am plucking hair out, hubby is in the bathroom mirror wishing he could grow some back.

I wish he could go through menopause.

Let's face it, no man dreams of Jeanie with the light brown hair.... on her upper lip and chin.

I tried laser hair removal at a fancy spa. $1,500 later the over-Botoxed, over-face-pulled lady told me, "Oh, it doesn't work on white or blond hair. You should try electrolysis."

What?

You could not tell me that $1,500 ago?

I spent weeks letting her zap me with a laser, which feels like someone snapping you with an elastic band, only to find out it does not work on light hair! I would have grabbed her by the short and curlys but from the dark brown hair on her head I got the feeling she did not have any.

I tracked down one of the few people in town who can do electrolysis. Believe me, you do not want to go to someone who doesn't know what they are doing. For $20 and 15 minutes, my new friend Debbie solved my facial hair problem in 4 weeks. Now I just go back for a touch up every month or so.

Keep in mind electrolysis is not pain free. She inserts a needle in the hair follicle and zaps it. It hurts a little more than plucking with tweezers but a lot less than being snapped with an elastic band. It also works on blond hair as well as dark. Now that Debbie has rid me of my chin hairs, she is doing my eyebrows and sideburns. Apparently, I am turning into Chewbacca in my old age.

Now you know what they say, "A hair on the chin is worth two in the bush." Debbie introduced me to the Brazilian. (This is where men should stop reading. You would not be able to take the pain.)

The Brazilian proved to me that I could survive Guantanamo Bay while laughing in the face of my captors.

Pain!

Women will put up with any kind of pain for beauty. Recently, before a trip down south, Debbie suggested I get a Brazilian. I had never had one before, but she assured me, "Everyone was doing it." She told me that most women take some kind of painkiller before having a Brazilian and some even bring a shot of alcohol with them to take before the process.

Now, I have had waxing done on my eyebrows and legs before. It is painful but I've also been through 12 hours of back labour. Nothing scares me. I laid on the table and she began to go to work. The bikini line was not that bad. Once the endorphins kicked in, I stopped feeling the pain. Until she got to the sensitive area. I cannot tell you what it feels like to have the hair ripped from the most sensitive part of your body.

When I thought she was finally finished she said, "Roll over on your side." I did as I was instructed. Before I had a chance to ask her what she was doing. She said, "This is where you and I become close friends." I felt the warm wax being spread from stem to stern. I looked like a deer in the headlights. Before I had a chance to say, "Stop," it was "wax on" "wax off." That is all I can say about that.

It is no longer uncomfortable now. We talk about our kids, vacations; she is wearing rubber gloves while spreading hot wax over my Who-ha with a Popsicle stick.

We never talk about politics or religion. That would be weird.

I do not want to split hairs, but everyone has their own pain level.

Let me describe the pain level... It is a real hair-raising experience.

Now, I have given birth twice and had a six-hour back surgery.

I know pain.

The first rip is like being kicked in the Who-ha. I cannot lie.

The second one is like hitting your cold toes on the corner of a table. By the time you are halfway through, the endorphins kick in and you can't feel anything. By the time it is over you just want to go home, roll up in a ball and rock for a while. The next day, you feel great and you book another appointment.

Ladies, this is something you do not want to try at home! The last thing you need is to be locked in your bathroom after pouring hot wax on yourself and chicken out. When that wax goes cold, it becomes sealing wax and closes all holes around it. You will have to call the Fire Department to help you out and they are going to need the Jaws of Life.

Although Debbie tells me she does her own Brazilian. Now that is a woman I would follow into battle.

Menopause has thrown me another curve ball, but Mother Nature is not winning this round. Not by the hair of my chinny, chin, chin. I will not be letting my hair down anytime soon.

I have made a second pact with my best friend Nancy, if we end up in a senior's home, we will pluck each other's chin hairs.

IS BEAUTY IN THE EYE OF THE SCALPEL HOLDER?

I admit, when I turned forty-five, I went to see a cosmetic surgeon.

Every night I was looking in the mirror wishing I could pull the skin under my eyes back a little bit and staple it in place.

I wanted to get a second opinion from a professional, so I booked an appointment. I did not tell my husband because I knew he wouldn't agree. I did not think I needed a lot of work done. I was not looking for a complete facelift. Just a nip and tuck here and there.

The doctor came in the room and put the magnifying glass over my face and examined all my fine lines and wrinkles.

He suggested I should have an eye lift just as a preventative measure. Maybe pull my cheeks back just a little bit. It would not hurt to have a little neck lift done and we could finish it off by plumping up my lips with injections.

It was quite a blow to my ego. I thought my face was fine.

I left the office disappointed because I was counting on this doctor to tell me I looked great for my age and did not need any work at all. On the way home I almost rear-ended a car while I was examining the bags under my eyes in the rear-view mirror. I decided to leave my face alone.

The funny thing is, I asked the doctor how many women my age came in for a consultation and he told me we were his main target audience. I then asked how many women bring their husbands to these appointments and he informed me it is rare for husbands to come to the appointment. I asked why; he whispered, "Because I've never met a husband who agreed their wife needed cosmetic surgery."

Then added, "Husbands are bad for business."

Why do we do it?

I don't disagree with plastic surgery. If I had the money, I would be a cross between Joan Rivers and Dolly Parton. If money were no object, I'd have everything nipped, tucked, sucked, and stapled back in place. I think plastic surgery is a good thing.

I had a friend who had what is referred to as a "Witches nose." She had the nickname "Witchy Poo" since kindergarten. Her nose became the focus of her life. She had spent her life trying to hide it, cover it, and God forbid if you took a picture of it. When she was in her thirties, she had a nose job. It completely changed her life. She was way more outgoing. She was open to relationships and within six months of her surgery she met her husband. Her life completely changed. The real problem was her self-esteem. It was as plain as the nose on her face. The nose job gave her self-confidence. I think it was the best money she ever spent.

Every fifteen minutes, there is a celebrity on TV telling me how to lose weight. But what is wrong with being a little overweight? Do we all have to be twigs? I know there's the obvious health reasons, but you can be healthy and a little overweight. Whatever happened to being pleasantly plump? And is food the real reason we carry all that extra baggage around our waist?

I ran into a friend from high school who used to be a teenage beauty queen. I hardly recognized her. Her eyes looked vaguely familiar, but she was nowhere near the girl she used to be. We got to talking. She told me she had suffered three miscarriages in three years. Her mother died and it was a devastating loss to her. Then after years of trying for a child, her husband left her. I felt bad for judging her. My first thought was, "She really let herself go," but after a ten-minute conversation, I realized the extra weight was protective coating to keep her from feeling pain. She did not need a celebrity telling her how easy it is to lose the pounds. She needed her heart mended.

How quick we are to judge each other.

As women, we will try the craziest things to achieve a standard of beauty that we know is unreachable. I once wore three pairs of Spanx under a dress. I sat through a full three course meal, a dance, and five hours of socializing. When I got home and took the Spanx off, it was like cutting open a bag of insulation. I am surprised my internal organs didn't fail.

Who doesn't love beauty tips? I will try anything once.

A friend of mine who is a successful model swears that Preparation H is the best eye cream on the market. She explained that the cream shrinks and tightens hemorrhoids. Therefore, she puts it around her eye before she goes to bed. I tried it and it works!

Another friend told me that she uses sugar every second night to clean her face with. It exfoliates your skin. Her face looks great. She also said she takes a sugar shower once a week. She takes a cupful of sugar in the shower and exfoliates her whole body. I tried it and your skin feels amazing afterwards.

My mother says the best thing for your skin is draining boiled potatoes. When she drains potatoes, she puts her face over the steam. This also works.

Another friend of mine told me her secret to great skin is baby oil. When she gets out of the shower, she rubs baby oil all over her body while it is still wet, then pats herself dry with a towel. The oil locks the moisture into the skin. It must work because she looks great.

Beauty is a billion-dollar business. I am afraid to add up how much I have contributed to that total. After everything I put myself through, it is funny that my husband thinks I look best with no makeup on at all.

If plastic surgeons think husbands are bad for business, and husbands like us without makeup. Then who are we doing this for?

The truth is women do not dress up for men. We dress up for other women.

We spend an outrageous amount on a purse, but I have yet to hear a man say, "Look at the purse on her!"

Men like things simple, which is why magazines called "Cars" and "Boobs" exist.

Women like things complicated, which is why Harlequin Romance novels exist.

We need the perfect dress, the perfect shoe, the perfect purse; we plan the whole night days ahead of time. We stay awake at night planning the details in our heads. We drive ourselves crazy trying to achieve a level of perfection that does not exist. Men hit the pillow and fall asleep within thirty seconds, dreaming of cars and boobs. Which is why they live longer.

If beauty is in the eye of the beholder, then today, let's be our own holders! Let's pretend every street and hallway is our catwalk, then work it girl, because we are beautiful!

WHO DO YOU LOVE MORE, MOMMY OR DADDY?

Ah come on! You all know it is Mommy.

Google "Songs about parents." For every song about fathers, there are ten about mothers. We rule!

As the old saying goes, "The hand that rocks the cradle is the hand that rules the world."

Not that we are better parents than men. We just parent differently than men do.

Men, on the other hand, will live a lot longer than us because they don't stress about the little things like we do. Men know how to relax.

I am standing at the kitchen counter making lunches for the next day, making sure everything is in the backpack for my daughter's day camp, and hubby is sitting in the TV room in the recliner, flipping between golf and race car driving.

He yells out, "Do you need any help?"

"Yes," I yell back.

"What do you want me to do?" Okay, so now I have to make a list... it's easier to just do it myself.

"Empty the garbage in the kitchen," I tell him.

"Okay." Then I wait five minutes. No sign of movement. I poke my head into the TV room. "Are you going to empty the garbage?"

"Yes, right after this ends." And that's how you press my anger/frustration button which plays all the curse words I know.

Women need it done now! Men need it done "right after this ends."

Hubby and I adjusted our workday when the kids were younger to accommodate their school day. I worked from 7 AM to 3 PM so I could be there when my son got home from school to get homework done with him before my two-year-old daughter came home to interrupt, and to make supper.

Hubby worked from 9 AM to 5 PM so he could get the kids up, fed, washed, and dropped off at day care and school on time, and he picks our daughter up on the way home. He handled the kids better in the morning and could get them out without fighting and I could handle them better in the afternoon because I didn't lose my temper over homework.

It worked out great and alleviated all the fighting about homework with a tired child and ensured we ate home cooked meals instead of fast food. I was more than impressed with my husband's efforts, especially when it came to doing our daughter's hair.

At two, her head was a mass of long curly locks that took forever to comb out and was the cause of many a tantrum. If she saw me even walk past with a brush, she would run from the room screaming. Somehow, he was able to tame her wild locks and get her to sit still for pigtails, ponytails, plaits, even a French braid. I was more than impressed – I was jealous! I couldn't do a French braid!

One week hubby had to go out of town on business and I did both the morning and the afternoon shift. I dreaded the thought of mornings. My daughter was not a morning person and I knew we were going to fight about those curly locks. Then, just as I had predicted, she saw me coming with the brush and the place went up.

An hour later I dragged her into day care. She was still sniffling from the morning cry and I looked like Alice Cooper with my mascara dripping down my face.

I took her coat off and brought her into the playroom. Sheila, her teacher, greeted us. She put her hand out and asked, "Where's the bag?" "Oh Jeez," I thought, "I forgot something."

"I am so frazzled today. What did I forget?" I asked.

"Her hair clips."

"What clips?" I asked.

Then she filled me in on hubby's dirty little secret, "Your husband can't do her hair, so he brings me a bag of clips and elastics every morning and I do her hair. I make her believe we are playing princess."

When hubby got home a few days later I asked him, "Show me how to do a French braid? I really want to learn." "No," he said, "I don't want to go at her hair now. She gets upset." "Really," I pressed, "then do it to my hair." "It wouldn't look good on you," he said.

"You're busted, buddy! Sheila told me that she does her hair!" The jig was up.

I wasn't mad, I was still impressed. Rather than start each day out with a fight, he found a way that let both of them have a good day. I would have pinned her to the floor and stapled bows in her head.

Who do you love more? I guess kids love their parents in different ways. It's not a competition… but they do love their mother more than anyone else.

Just saying.

IS CHIVALRY DEAD?

A Twitter friend of mine suggested I write a blog on chivalry.

Recently he held the door to let a lady walk through and she made a rude comment stating she can hold her own door. He didn't know what he did wrong.

Sometimes women believe chivalry is rooted in sexism and is outdated. That chivalry is based on women being the weaker sex. Really? Are we the weaker sex if a man holds the door for us? Or stands when we get up to leave a room? Pulls out a chair when we want to sit down or helps us put on our coat?

Or is chivalry simply good manners and good upbringing?

According to the dictionary, chivalry means the medieval system of knighthood; knightly qualities, bravery, courtesy, respect for women. Manners means polite social behaviour.

My friend is part of a generation that was told by his mother to open the door for a lady. I was raised in a generation that expects him to hold the door. I am always appalled when a man doesn't open the door for me. My first thought is, "Who raised him?"

Manners is a totally different thing. Manners is teaching your kids not to spit on the sidewalk or fart at the table. That's a totally different set of "raising" rules. I don't believe enough parents teach manners either.

I do teach my son to be chivalrous. It's not something I put on my "raising" priority list. It's something that comes naturally to me. Maybe I am turning into my mother, but when I am going somewhere with my son I always say, "Be a gentleman, go up ahead and hold the door please," or "Let the lady go ahead of you," or "Help your grandmother with her coat." I expect when I am not with him, he does this on his own. I would be upset if someone told me they saw my son walking into the mall and he slammed the door in a lady's face. I would also be upset if they said they saw him slam the door in a man's face.

I also apply the same rules to my daughter. I am always saying to her, "That is not very ladylike," and she says to me "Mom, you're the only one who says that!"

I don't care.

Telling her to "Sit up straight or don't chew with your mouth open," is just about manners and pride in yourself.

Both are warned not to spit in my presence or fart at the table. Manners are equally important for both sexes.

I like the way Catherine, Duchess of Cambridge, has brought being a lady back in vogue.

She was criticized by the media for wearing nylons with her dresses. Really? The horror! A young woman with class. How awful for the media. Wearing dresses that touch her knee! My God, how will they sell papers? Pearls, those pearls passed down from her mother, the tart! How dare she?

After a decade of Pop Princesses that drive drunk and show up at events with no underwear, Duchess Catherine is a welcome sight for mothers of teenage girls.

It is chivalry that reminds a man to hold the door for a lady and let her walk through. It is good manners to hold the door for your male friend. Either way it doesn't make you a bad person for doing it.

I met a friend at a coffee shop for lunch one day. At that time, I was recovering from back surgery. Having two titanium rods screwed into my spine had left me unable to walk without a cane for a while. I was new in the "disabled world" and learning how to manoeuvre around.

My friend had arrived before me and was sitting down with her meal. I went to the counter and ordered mine. Then I was told to go to the counter at the end to get my tray. I struggled, trying to keep my purse on my shoulder, lean on my cane, and balance my tray filled with hot coffee and soup.

There were several people standing around me and I couldn't help but notice they all looked at their shoes or the ceiling. Knowing they should do something but not sure what. A man sitting in the corner stood up and walked over. He said, "Missus, do you need some help?" He didn't wait for my answer and took the tray from my hand. While he walked me to my table he said to the crowd, "You see the lady needs help and not one of you would help her!" They all looked away.

My friend had her back to me and wasn't aware that I needed help. The funny thing was this man was the most unlikely knight in shining armour that I have ever met.

He was covered in tattoos, including a huge spider web that covered his entire face and several other works of art like skulls and crosses on his neck. If I had spotted him across the room, knightly qualities like bravery, courtesy and respect for women would not be adjectives I would have used on him. I would expect to see him on the nightly news being led into the courthouse in shackles. He certainly gave my friend a fright when she looked up and saw this man laying a tray down at her table. His taste in artwork was different than mine, but someone raised him right.

Was I insulted? No, I was thankful. I learned that knights come in all kinds of shining armour. Did it make me feel like a weak woman? No, not at all. I would hope my son would do the same thing. It just made me feel crappy for judging a knight by the cover of his armour.

My husband was an officer with the Navy and is a retired police officer. He is both an officer and a gentleman. Chivalry is second nature for him. For almost twenty years he has held doors for me and pulled out my chair at formal events (nightly meals at home don't count). He helps me with my coat always, but we are equals in our marriage.

Is chivalry sexist?

I hold open the door for ladies and men to let them go first. Am I sexist?

Listen, most women I know can kick your ass. There's nothing weak about them. Remember, Jane Fonda introduced us to aerobics years ago. We can mess you up bad.

We've been taking care of ourselves for years.

I think women who say things like, "I can hold my own door," are rude. Plain and simple.

It's just not ladylike behaviour.

LOST IN TRANSLATION

I am dialing my third 1-800 number. I bought a GE fridge from Sears in October and the darn door keeps breaking on it.

Yesterday I opened the door to get low-fat, Greek yogurt, which I eat before having McDonalds to make myself feel better. The fridge door starts doing the old bump and grind but not in a good way. I closed the door and heard the same sound. I continue to open and close it, hoping the sound would go away, but it just gets worse.

I started looking around the hinges, hoping I can fix it, to no avail. I closed the door and walked away, hoping when I came back later for the low-fat, chocolate pudding it would have fixed itself.

But it didn't. I pull out the warranty card and the receipt from Sears and call the overly friendly lady who sold me the fridge. She's not that friendly now, or that helpful. She gives me a 1-800 number to call. I call it to find out there's another 1-800 number to call. I continuously press 1 for English… 1 for service, 1 for repairs, 1 for appliances and 1 for fridges. I get rewarded with elevator music. My marketing mind is wondering why they are not playing the soundtrack to Frozen instead.

Finally, "Paul" with the East Indian accent answers

only to tell me I have to call back the first 1-800 number I was given because they take care of the issue if the fridge is less than one year old.

I start the process again: 1-800, press 1 for English, 1 for service, 1 for appliances, 1 for fridges, five minutes of elevator music. How ironic the first song is Eric Carmen's "All by Myself".

Finally Sue, with her thick East Indian accent, answers the phone with, "Please tell me your phone number?" I go into the whole here's my name & number spiel.

Then she asks me why I am calling so I go through the whole "My fridge door is broke" routine for the third time.

Then she asks me, "What is the closest major intersection near your home?"

"What? I am not sure what you just said," I tell her.

"Please tell me the name of the closest major intersection near your home." I get this feeling that she is going to tell me to go play in it.

"Why? What's that got to do with my fridge door?"

"I have to be able to tell the repair man how to find your house," she tells me.

Now I decide to have some fun with her. "I live next door to Andrea. You know Andrea? We worked together years ago. She's blond, likes gardening."

There's a long pause. "I don't know Andrea. I need the name of the closest major intersection."

"Toronto."

"Okay, thank you. Do you have a dog?"

It went over her head. "Yes, I have a dog."

"Okay then. You will have to be good to your dog."

"I am always good to my dog."

"The dog has to be taken care of."

"My dog is treated better than most children. Why are you asking about my dog? Do you think he broke the fridge?"

"No. When our repair man arrives you will have to take care of the dog."

"I will send the dog to the spa for the day. He will be happy Sears is so concerned about him."

"We have to make sure the dog does not get angry at the repair man."

"Oh," then I get it. "The dog will be fine. I am the one pissed at the repair man. This is his second trip to fix the door."

With a straight voice she says, "We cannot send a repair man if you're going to be angry with him."

"I won't be angry with him. I'll take care of him like the dog."

"What?" she asks

"I'll be as good to the repair man as I am to my dog," my fingers are crossed but she can't see that.

"Okay, I will give you a file number and the phone number to a local repair man."

"What? I have to call another number? Why can't you make the appointment?"

"Oh, we can't make the appointment. You have to call a local repair man to set up the appointment."

"Okay, give me the number."

"902-753…"

"Wait. 902 is Nova Scotia. I am calling from Newfoundland."

"Yes, that is fine. Call this number and they will send a repair man to you within two days," she reassures me.

"Not from Nova Scotia. I need a repair man in Newfoundland."

"No, this is the number you have to call. They will drive to your house in two days."

"I doubt that. I live on an Island. They have to fly or take a ferry. I need a number that starts with 709."

"Okay. I do have a number that starts with 709, but you have to call the other number first. I assure you the repair man will come to your house very quickly."

"Is that because he knows my dog will be locked away at the spa and I have to be nice to him?"

Another long pause. "Do you have a pen?"

"Yes, I have a pen. Give me the number."

Then she adds, "Are you happy with our service? Is there anything else I can do for you?"

"Do you dog sit? The spa is expensive for the whole day."

Giggles. "No, we don't dog sit."

I hang up the phone and call the local number… 1 for service… 1 for appliances… 1 for fridges…. elevator music… finally a female voice…. "Can I have your ticket number?"

I read it out to her. "When did you buy your fridge?"

"In October."

"Okay. We don't fix the fridges that are less than one year old. You have to dial this number: 1-800…."

She rambles off the same 1-800 I just hung up from.

"I just spoke to them and they said to call you." My voice is still nice because I don't want to be put on the "Bitch" list and have to wait for weeks.

"Okay. I'll take your name and number and check with GE, but I don't think we can take this call."

I give her my information. I should have taken the Nova Scotia number to see if they really would have been here in two days.

I open the door and the grinding sounds louder. I start searching around for anything that's not low-fat. I spot a plate of left-over sausages and Minnie, my dog, starts to whine for one.

"Oh, shut up," I tell her, "and if you think you're getting a frigging spa day out of this you're mad. I am locking you in the garage."

I bite into a cold sausage and dial 1-800...1 for English... 1 for service... 1 for appliances... 1 for fridges... elevator music.... It's Dan with his East Indian accent, "Please give me your name, address and state your problem please."

"Queen Elsa of Arendelle. My magic powers are gone. I can't seem to freeze anything because my fridge is broken."

"Do you have a dog?"

"No, a reindeer, his name is Sven. He can't fly but he is friendly."

Long pause.... He mutters something in East Indian... then the dial tone.

Dan hung up on me and I don't know why. We were having such a good time.

LOST AT THE MALL: THE DAY YOUR MOTHER DIES

When I was about seven years old, I went to the shopping mall with my mother. We would always start at Woolco.

She took me to the toy department and let me play while she shopped. After about twenty minutes of exploring the toy department I decided to go look for her. I walked through the store, looking up and down every aisle like I was crossing the street, but I couldn't find her.

I searched the store, but she was nowhere to be found. I thought I spotted her in the shoe department. I ran towards her but realized as I got close, it was a lady with a similar coat. I began to panic and started to run faster through store, calling out to her. I circled the store one more time and still no sign of her.

Panic turned to fear as I realized I was lost, and tears began to flow. The tears were blurring my sight and I couldn't breathe. I tried calling out, "Mom, mom," but the only thing that could escape from my throat was a dry, heavy gulp of tears.

A saleslady stopped me and asked if I was lost. I tried to say yes but I could barely breathe from the heavy sobs coming from my chest. All I could do was nod yes. She brought me to the customer service desk and as we got closer, I could see my mother talking to the lady behind the counter and ran towards her. I couldn't get a word out of my throat. She saw me coming and I flew into her arms.

She said, "Where were you? I've been looking for you everywhere!"

My face was soaking from tears and snot that left train tracks on my cheeks and chin. She took a tissue from her coat pocket and dried my face. All I could get out was one word at a time between heavy sobs. "I thought you left me," I cried.

"You know I'd never leave you," she sighed.

She took me by the hand, and we went to the restaurant, sat down, and had custard cones until I calmed down.

That feeling of being lost at Woolco came back to me this week, when my sister called to say mom, who had been sick for a while, had been admitted to hospital and wasn't doing well.

As I drove towards the hospital, that feeling of panic and fear that I felt as a seven-year-old lost in a store came back to me. When I ran across the parking lot the tears were blurring my sight and I wanted to call out, "Mom, mom," but the only thing that could escape from my throat was a dry, heavy gulp of tears.

I rode the elevator to the seventh floor and took a wrong turn. I ended up on the opposite end of the hospital. I stopped at the nursing station and told the nurse at the desk I was looking for my mother. She brought me to her room.

When I got there, she was frail and weak. I took her by the hand and said, "I got lost when I got off the elevator and couldn't find you." My face was soaking from tears and snot that left train tracks on my cheeks and chin. She held a tissue in her hand, and she dried my face. All I could get out was one word at a time between heavy sobs. "I thought you left me," I cried.

"You know I'd never leave you," she sighed.

I took her hand but this time I knew we were not going for ice cream. I knew this time would be the last time she found me.

At eighty-five, her various health problems had caught up with her.

The heart that had given decades of unconditional love was failing her. I was able to spend an hour with her by myself before the army of children, grand-children, and great-grand-children showed up.

We got to say good-bye.

Today she closed her eyes and went to sleep, and I cried like a seven-year-old lost at Woolco who knew she would never be found again.

I love you, Mom.

ME A HOARDER?

I admit it. I am a clothes hoarder... and a shoe hoarder... a purse hoarder... and jewelry.

That's all. That's all I hoard. I swear.

We've been married over twenty years and hubby still only has one drawer in the bedroom. I keep telling him it's because I haven't decided if I am keeping him or not.

Truth is, I have every drawer and closet in the house bursting with stuff. I am afraid to answer the door when the bell rings because it could be the A&E network bursting in to do an intervention and force me on that Hoarding show.

I not only have my closet full, but I have my daughter's closet full, and I just put two big closets in the upstairs hall to hold my suits and dresses!

Shoes! I AM the old lady who lived in the shoe! I am afraid to count how many pairs I have.

Every week I buy more! Not just for me but for my kids, too.

A few weeks ago, I decided enough is enough. It's time to get that hoarding monkey off my back. I took a box of those big orange industrial-size garbage bags and decided to clean out the closets.

Rule number one: If I haven't worn it in the last year,

it has to go.

Rule number two: If it's older than my children, it has to go.

Rule number three: Unless it's a wedding dress or a christening gown, clothes do not have sentimental value.

Fill those bags!

I realized as I was going through my stuff my closets had become a museum to the 80s, 90s and 2000s.

I did well. I threw out all my Lady Diana blouses (the ones with the lace collar and black string tie). Notice I said "Lady" Diana, not "Princess" Diana. My blouses even predate her royal title.

A white leather mini skirt (What the hell was I thinking?). I wore that to the Tina Turner concert at St. John's Memorial Stadium with shiny black leather four-inch heels and fishnet nylons. I used a full can of Aqua Net to hold my Tina look-a-like hairdo in place. Now that I think about it, I looked more like a drag queen imitating Tina. Because of the 80s, there's a hole in the ozone layer with my name on it.

Jeans in size twelve, ten, nine, eight and even a six! Yes, like Oprah, I am every woman or at least I've been every size over the past thirty years. I even found a pair of Jordache jeans that I remember dancing in to Wham's "Wake Me Up Before You Go-Go" at Club Max.

There was a pair of Calvin Kleins. Apparently, nothing comes between me and my Calvin's, not even a few decades. And of course, the pièce de résistance – the jeans with the hundreds of rips up and down the legs. The ones that would send my mother into a complete tizzy!

Maternity clothes, like I was ever going to wear them again!

Painting clothes, like I was ever going to wear them

again!

Halfway through my closet the decade changes to the 90s. I remember having "The Rachel" haircut like every other girl on George Street.

I did find a pair of jean overalls that I wore everywhere!

And yes, I did wear them with one strap undone. I remember dancing up George Street to "Come on Eileen" in those.

In the back of the basement closet I found my red Doc Martens. I bought them in Toronto around 1991. I was too cool for school in these beauties. I wore them with Madonna lace skirts, my Gloria Vanderbilt jeans, dresses, bike shorts, you name it. If these boots could talk, I would have to put them in a witness protection program. Now they're on their way to the Salvation Army. It's like giving a friend away.

My closets are like a tribute to musical history. Directly influenced by Tina Turner, Madonna, Wham, and every other artist that made the 80's and 90's fun.

My clothes made a drastic change around the late 90s and into the 2000s. That's when I supposedly grew up. I had children and went from a party girl to a professional lady.

Mini skirts changed to respectable suits, and four-inch heels and Doc Martens were sent to the downstairs closet to make way for sleeker, more professional shoes. The fishnets were thrown out to make way for control top pantyhose. My jeans turned darker with no rips or patches. Suddenly I had a closet of "Big girl" clothes.

It took two days to clean out my closet and my children's. In all, eight big orange garbage bags were carted off to the Salvation Army. Eight big bags of memories, bad decisions, impulse buys, and "I once looked hot in that" items were sent off to a place where other people will get a chance to wear them.

I couldn't help but wonder how much all that stuff cost me over the years. There are probably thousands of dollars in those bags. Some of it may still be on my credit card statement.

It's time to let the 80s and the 90s go and die in peace.

I imagine that some afternoon I will be driving downtown, and a homeless person will cross the street in front of my car. She'll be wearing my red Doc Martens, ripped Calvin Kleins and lace Madonna top. I'll roll down the window and scream to the top of my lungs, "YOU GO GIRL! YOU LOOK HOT! THE 80s ROCK!"

MOM DOESN'T HAVE A PENIS!

We stopped at a gas station/restaurant on the side of the highway while on our way to a short vacation. We were driving to Gander with our three-year-old son Daniel.

Hubby went to the restaurant side to get us a table and I took our son to the Ladies room with me to pee. The bathroom was full of ladies. We huddled into the small stall and I let him go first. He was getting the hang of standing up to pee. To keep his aim on target I always kept Cheerios in a baggy in my purse. I would throw a few in the toilet and tell him to sink the Cheerios. He was enormously proud of his perfect aim.

After I pulled his pants up, I said, "You stand there now and be a good boy, mom has to pee, too."

"Do you want me to throw the Cheerios in, mom?"

"No. Moms don't need Cheerios," I told him.

"Because you got good aim, right?"

I could hear the ladies outside the stall giggle at him.

I squat down to pee and a look of shock and horror came over his little three-year-old face. "Where's your penis, mom?" he asked with all sincerity. The ladies outside the stall were in a full roar by now.

"Shush!" I told him. "Be quiet, the ladies can hear you!"

"Your penis is gone! How are you peeing?" He bent down, trying to look for my penis. The ladies outside could barely get their breath by now and I was trying rush my pee and pull my pants up without having to explain the birds and the bees in a gas station bathroom stall.

I opened the stall door. The ladies were waiting to see the innocent face of my three-year-old.

"Does dad know you don't have a penis?" His questions persisted, even at the sink as I washed his hands.

"Yes, he knows. Girls don't have penises. Be quiet," I tried to rush him out of the room.

I could hear the laughter hit the ceiling as I exited the washroom.

While I was adjusting my clothes on the way to our table he got out of my grip and started running through the restaurant. He spotted his father sitting at the furthest table away from us. As soon as his little feet hit the floor he yelled out in his loudest voice, "Dad, dad, dad!!! Mom lost her penis! She doesn't have a penis!"

The whole restaurant erupted into laughter while turning to see this blue-eyed toddler running towards his father. My husband froze, not sure what he was hearing, and by the time it registered with him, it was too late. Our son was at the table and jumping up in a chair.

Our son looked his father right in the eye and said, "Mom left her penis at home. She had to pee sitting down!" Unable to hold back his laugh, hubby informed him, "Girls don't have penises. God didn't give them any. That's okay. Now lower your voice."

My three-year-old then spotted me walking towards the table, aware that every eye in the place was looking at me. He yelled out, "Mom! That's okay. You didn't lose your penis. God didn't give you one."

Red-faced, I sat at the table. A waitress arrived at the same time with a big bowl of chocolate ice cream. She sat it down in front of him.

'We didn't order this," I told her.

"I know," she said, "but this little guy made me laugh today like I haven't laughed in years. He deserves a big bowl of chocolate ice cream."

"You're the prettiest waitress I've ever seen," he said with a big chocolate smile. She thanked him and we received service equal to any five-star restaurant.

Every patron in the place came by to say hello to the little boy who made them laugh and the Mom who didn't have a penis.

MY MOTHER SAYS THE STRANGEST THINGS

My mother says the strangest things. Let me tell you about a few.

I was watching the evening news one night with her and the top two stories were about recent murders.

The first story was about an estranged husband who had shot his wife. After the story aired, my mother responded with complete contempt and muttered, "That bastard! God only knows what that poor woman had to live with. The years of abuse she suffered." In that brief three-minute news story, she had imagined the victim's whole life and the hardship of living with this man.

The next story was about a woman who had stabbed her common-law husband to death. My mother continued to rock back and forth in her recliner, intently listening to the details, but she didn't comment. The look on her face said she was thinking deeply about something. I waited for a few minutes before I said anything. I couldn't help but to speak up and ask, "You were so outraged at the first story about the man killing the woman, but you didn't say anything about the woman killing the man. Why?"

She looked directly at me with a twinkle in her blue eyes and grinned, "I was just sitting here wondering what that bastard did to piss her off enough that she had to kill him. He must have been bugging her all day."

"If you ever get selected for jury duty please let me know so I can talk to them first," I told her.

The world has changed in eighty-five years and my mother had a hard time keeping up with it. She always worked from home. She believed hard work reaped great benefits. She has never used a fax machine or email. She's convinced Facebook will be the downfall of this generation. "Talking about your private lives on a computer, my God, what are the young ones thinking?" she implored.

She thinks LOL is "lots of love." She left me a message that said, "Helen, I can't find the cat. I am worried she is dead somewhere. LOL Mom"

She called me one day at work and asked me to take her to Zellers. She wanted to go shopping and, of course, she had to return something (most times without the bill). I was convinced she bought items she didn't need for the sole purpose of returning them.

I told her I just couldn't get up in the middle of a workday and pick her up to go shopping. I explained that I now reported to a higher power and not one that walked on water. Leaving in the middle of the day when you weren't on a stretcher wasn't acceptable.

"Tell your boss you have a doctor's appointment," she said. "I can't. I have to give 24 hours notice for a doctor's appointment."

"Then tell him you have to do something for your mother." "It doesn't work that way," I told her. She was relentless, "I'll write a note saying you had to leave early to help me. Will that work?"

Unable to hold back the laughs, knowing her mind wondered back to my school days, I answered, "No, that won't work on him but write the note anyway. I just want to see the look on his face when I hand it in."

It was a simpler time when she could just write a note to say, "Dear Sister, Helen was sick yesterday. Please forgive her. Mrs. Cleary." When I really stayed home so we could go shopping downtown and end the day by having cherry pie at Bowring's restaurant while we looked at the ships in the harbour, guessing where they came from and where they were going next.

In her younger days, my mother looked like Elizabeth Taylor's younger sister. She was almost six foot tall, thin, with long black hair that she kept in a beehive on top of her head. When I came home from school on cold winters days with cold hands, she would let me put them in her beehive to warm them. She wore black pencil skirts and crisp, starched white blouses, pearls, and perfume. No one loves perfume like my mother. I always knew when mom was going out in the evening when I could smell the Chanel No. 5 ten miles away.

My mother always has an interesting take on things. I asked her if she watched the Octomom reality show when it first aired. "No," she scoffed, "I had ten kids. I am Octomom and I did it without lights and cameras! I could make a chicken feed ten kids and turn the leftovers into a soup!" She could too.

I remember mashed potato sandwiches and putting Carnation milk on bread sprinkled with sugar as a snack.

She once called me to say, "Helen, my friend is turning ninety this weekend. What should I get her, I wonder?" Jokingly I replied, "A coffin." She huffed back at me, "Don't be so foolish, she already has one. She bought it twenty years ago." I pointed out, "See, that's the difference between my friends and yours. Mine don't own their coffins yet." "Yes," she informed me, "my friends are just hitting the diaper stage again."

I could never trust her in front of my friends; she seems to have selective amnesia when it's convenient. One afternoon we ran into my old boyfriend at the mall. "Mom, do you remember (I won't use his name to protect the guilty)?" She puts on her glasses, "I wouldn't know you now. You used to be really good looking. What happened to you?" I try to hurry her out the door. "You dodged a bullet there, Helen." "He can still hear you, Mom, and you're the one who wouldn't let him go, not me."

She has spent most of her life alone, choosing to work herself to death than marrying again. I asked her one time, "Mom, you should go to the Legion and meet men your age. It would be nice to have someone to do things with." She scoffed. "I am eighty-three! Any man I meet now will be wearing diapers. I'd rather be strapped to a horse's arse and shit to death!" Point taken.

I have learned that I get my sense of humour from her. She gets hers from years of choosing laughter over pain and finding the "funny" in everything around her. Her life was hard and horrific at times, but her sense of humour kept her going.

She died in 2012. I still miss her every day. I remember her smile the most and her laugh. Maybe that's the secret to a long life: laugh. Laugh at everything.

WHAT'S REAL ABOUT THE REAL HOUSEWIVES OF ANYWHERE?

A friend told me I had to watch the Real Housewives reality show. These types of shows have never interested me. I don't watch TV for reality. I live that every day. I watch TV for fantasy. I want to believe Tom Selleck really is the police commissioner of New York and Olivia Pope is sleeping with the President of the United States.

But I did give the Real Housewives a try.

I watched two episodes from two different cities. I don't get it! I just don't get why women watch this. Or better yet, why do they idolize them?

I have a lot of female friends and although we all do our share of gossiping, I can honestly say I have never punched one in the face or tore a friend's wig off at the country club.

How can this be real?

The plot is always the same:

Part 1: Two or three of them meet to backstab the one who is not there.

Part 2: The other one finds out and vows revenge.

Part 3: They all break to go shopping for things none of them can really afford.

Part 4: They go to a public place (restaurant, country club, wedding).

Part 5: The fight breaks out. Husbands tear them apart, they get kicked out of the public place, police are called, etc.

During the episode I watched, they all go to a swanky restaurant for supper. The odd girl out discovers the other three have been talking trash about her. The screaming starts. Apparently, they don't notice the other diners in the restaurant and the camera man is too busy filming to give them the heads up.

I can only guess that the other diners are extras on the set because I can't imagine any upscale restaurant that would allow this to be filmed or take place while their regular paying clientele are eating.

Then a housewife grabs the other one by the hair and the fight breaks out. The main gossip girl, wearing Louboutin stilettos, lifts her knee and smashes it into the other's face.

Designer clothes are being ripped from their skeletal frames, silicone lips are being smashed (no blood runs), pumped up breast enhancements are being punched like fighting balloons, and bleach blond weaves are torn from their heads. The fur is flying... literally.

No one goes to hospital, only to emergency beauty salon appointments and plastic surgeons.

Now, I am not saying grown women don't fight. As a matter of fact, I did have an argument with a friend one time while having supper with her. We left miffed at each other and didn't talk for three weeks. I did think about unfriending her on Facebook but changed my mind. Not much of a show here. Move along people.

This show franchise makes grown women look shallow and trashy. It's the "16 and Pregnant" for thirty to sixty-year-olds.

I just hope to Jesus none of my friends start acting like

these women! Can you imagine me and my best friend, Nancy, at a restaurant and she finds out I said something nasty about her? Then she grabs my hair and I punch her in the face. We fall over tables, while diners give us dirty looks.

For the record, we are both from Freshwater Road, so this fight could go on all night. Especially if we have been drinking.

You know, all women in Canada only earned the right to vote in 1960. In 1918 government gave the right to vote to Canadian women twenty-one years of age and older, but most women of colour – including Chinese, East Indian and Japanese women – weren't allowed to vote at the provincial and federal level until the late 1940s. Aboriginal women covered by the Indian Act couldn't vote for band councils until 1951 and couldn't vote in federal elections until 1960.

In 1960 all women in Canada could vote.

Fast forward to today. Now we watch other women, injected with silicone, with tied-back faces, bitch-slap each other with designer bags on a weekly basis. Have you noticed there isn't any "Husbands of Beverly Hills?" Of course not.

Women have fought extremely hard for everything from the right to help choose our governments to the right to equal pay for equal work. Take a good look at these shows and ask yourself: "Is that what we fought for? Is that what I want my daughter's life to be like?"

We earned our vote. Let's use it wisely. Let's all vote to watch TV programs that portray women playing a lead role that empowers, inspires, and teaches them to be leaders and shows that let us believe Tom Selleck is the real Commissioner of the NYPD.

MY SON, THE POLITICIAN

Over the years, my son has wanted to be everything from a garbage man to a fighter pilot.

This week, he floored us when he announced he wanted to be... a politician!

We were devastated. As much as I hated the idea of him flying fighter planes through enemy territory, I would rather that over him being a politician!

I tried to explain that politics is a second-choice career. You have to get your education, build a career, retire, and then become a politician. Go out into the real world and get some life experience. Be successful at something. Then you can put your name on the ballot.

I should've seen this coming. I remember when he was about two years old. He would take all the cushions off the couch and pile them up on top of one another to make a podium. He would climb to the top of the pile and give passionate speeches. He would break into a sweat theatrically using hand gestures to make his points. I thought he was going to be a great lawyer and was practising his closing arguments as he brought criminals to justice. A politician needs charisma to deliver speeches that inspire people, and his charismatic charm was evident since he was a toddler.

He has ideals of how he is going to change the world in ways that no one before him ever could. I told him he must be reasonable. You can't change the world overnight. You must be realistic. You have to listen to people and understand the problems.

I thought back to when he was in grade four. He was small for his age and never a big eater.

Every day at school he ordered the same thing for lunch: a hamburger and chocolate milk.

Halfway through the year, he asked if he could order two hamburgers and two chocolate milk. I asked why; he said he was hungry. My mother's intuition kicked in and I began to wonder if he was being bullied or if somebody was taking his lunch money. So, I sat him down one night and told him I knew something was up. I demanded to know who was stealing his money or his lunch.

After a short period of denial, he confessed. He wasn't being bullied. He told me the boy who sat next to him often came with no lunch or money because his mother would forget.

My son took it upon himself to quietly solve the problem by ordering two lunches every day and sharing it with his schoolmate. I asked him if the teacher knew about it. He said he didn't want the teacher to know. I explained that adults need to get involved in a situation like this for reasons he could not understand. He told me that's why he didn't tell me because he knew I would make a big deal out of it. I tried to explain again that we have a duty to alert authorities at school to look out for the welfare of this child.

He said, "Mom, he was hungry, and I fed him. The problem is solved, now leave it alone. No one needs to know." Looking back, I realize how reasonable and realistic he was. He knew how to listen and understand people's problems and he did change this boy's world overnight without fanfare or accolades.

A politician must have integrity. He must be able to stand up for what he believes in. Even when it may not be popular with those around him. I knew as soon as I wrote that it was a moot point because I know my son has integrity. When he was in grade five, he got detention one day. I was surprised because he is a good student who never spoke back. He was very respectful.

I asked him what happened, and he told me there was a hearing-impaired student in his class. She was trying to change the batteries in her hearing aid while the teacher was talking, and it was interrupting the class. The teacher told her to stop making noise and to go outside the classroom to fix her batteries.

Flustered and embarrassed, the student began to cry and the faster she tried to fix the problem the more flustered she became. My son got up, walked across the classroom, took the hearing aid, and began to help her put the batteries in. The teacher yelled at him to sit back down and mind his own business. He said, "She needs help." The teacher told him again to sit down. He continued to help her take the batteries out of her hearing aid and replace them with new ones. Then he sat down. The teacher gave him detention for not listening to her. When he told me the story, I didn't believe him. I phoned the teacher and asked her, she gave me the exact same story. I told her, don't ever give my son detention again. He had no problem standing up for something he believed in, even if it meant getting detention.

I told him that politicians need fiscal experience and to be honest. But I knew he had no trouble there either. In kindergarten, my husband and I got called in by his teacher. She told us he had been taking money from his classmates.

We were both shocked. She called him into the classroom, and we asked him to explain what was going on. He had been asking for months to go to Disney World. We told him that it was expensive, and we couldn't afford it that year because we just had a baby, his sister. He decided to raise the money on his own.

He created coupons on loose leaf paper and wrote "ten cents" on each one. He cut them out and talked his classmates into buying the coupons. He was making a tidy profit by the time the teacher found out. She demanded he give the money back, but he refused, telling her this is "His new business", his "Coupon factory." She took the money and the coupons and called us in.

She asked him, "Do you know what you did wrong?" He said, "I didn't do anything wrong. I created my own business."

She was frustrated and she looked toward us for support. She said, "He's defiant. He refuses to admit what he did was wrong." We left the classroom and went out and sat in our car, not knowing what to say to each other. My husband looked at me and said, "What do we do?" I said, "Bring him to university, he's obviously ready for business school!"

We should have known then that we were raising a politician. Now that I think back over his life. I'm not surprised that he wants to go into politics. He's a born statesman with an innate sense of integrity, honesty, and charisma.

He plans on running in the next election. He tells me, "Don't worry, mom, I'm well-informed when it comes to politics." I tell him, "Then you'll definitely be elected because voters don't understand it at all!"

TWEETING IN THE 80'S

Thank God we didn't have social media when we were teenagers!

We are the last generation that can lie to our kids about our teenage years. Why? Because we didn't have Facebook or Twitter.

We didn't keep a daily running log of how much we hated school, who we had a crush on, who we didn't like, where we went or what we did.

We didn't take selfies ten times a day showing off our duck lips or take pictures of our lunch to show everyone how great our peanut butter sandwich looked in the wax paper.

No, we didn't drink when we were teenagers! We never spoke back to teachers; we treated them with the utmost respect. I never smoked a cigarette in my life. I was home every night by seven o'clock, except on Fridays and Saturdays when I could stay out till nine.

What! You don't believe your own mother!!! Prove it. Show me the evidence… that's right. There isn't any because my generation never had to deal with social media or the internet!

Google meant going to the library. Inviting people to your birthday party meant knocking on their front door and handing them an invitation that you wrote by hand.

Expanding your knowledge meant reading a book.

Thank God, too! Can you image if Facebook and Twitter existed when we were teens?

Still, I can't help but think... what if social media DID exist back in the 80s? What would a week of my Tweets and Facebook updates look like?

Let's see....

Monday morning:

"Attention Holy Heart High School gals, Sister Furey & the Penguins are on patrol – hide your smokes in your leg warmers."

Monday night:

"Dance at Heart Gym Friday night with the Brother Rice boys. Hide your flask in the lining of your purse. Mr. Byrd will never look there."

Tuesday morning:

"2 for 1 at Club Max this Friday night. Can't wait to disco! Got the biggest shoulder pads you've ever seen from Dalmys in Atlantic Place. Looks like I fell off the set of Dynasty. Will post a selfie later."

Tuesday lunch time:

"Sr. Furey forgot to pluck her chin hairs today. Like, grody to the max!"

Wednesday morning:

"Are you supposed to mix Lemon Gin with anything? Been throwing up yellow gall since Saturday night. So grossed out."

Wednesday after school:

"Crazy Bart just asked me out! Like, I am sure! Like, did you see his mullet? Gag me with a spoon."

Thursday morning:

"Picked up the latest Tiger Beat last night. Jon Bon Jovi is on the cover; he has a bodacious bod. No one is asking him "Where's the beef?""

Thursday evening:

"Loves Princess Diane's black ribbon tie on her frilly blouse. Can't wait to copy that Friday night for the dance. I am going to be so Bitchin'. Still don't know what she sees in Big Ears."

Friday morning:

"The corner store is selling smokes 3 for 25 cents. Anyone want to go in on a butt & a half with me?"

Friday lunch time:

"Dying for a Du Maurier extra light and Pepsi. Can't wait for school to end."

Saturday night:

"In the lineup at Club Max. Airhead in front of me is wearing a skirt to her knees. Like, barf me out. Who does she think she is, Olivia Neutron Bomb?"

5 minutes later:

"Mall chick standing behind us in the line is freakin' because our cigarette smoke is blowing in her face. Like, don't have a cow, lame ass. It's a free world!"

5 minutes after that:

"Dipstick on the door is checking for IDs. Brenda is shitting bricks. I told her take a chill pill. We're totally rad."

20 minutes later:

"Finally in. Fixed our faces and we're already on the dance floor. Can't wait to show off my Moon Walk."

20 Minutes later:

"Some dudes are doing the Worm in the middle of the dance floor. This place is totally off the grid!"

Last Tweet:

"Word up! We're totally baffed. On the way home."

Ya, I am so glad Facebook and Twitter were not invented in the 80s. My children will never know how cool I really was.

Word to ya mother.

OBSERVATIONS IN THE MALL: THE LADY WITH THE EXPENSIVE PURSE

I was standing in the checkout line at the Dollar Store in the mall. I had a basket full of decorations for my daughter's birthday party.

There was a young lady standing in front of me; she was next to get checked in.

Her hair was blond, perfectly straight. It fell just below her shoulders. Her long white coat came just above her knee. The hem of the blue dress she was wearing fell about an inch below the coat to reveal tanned legs. She was over-dressed for the Dollar Store. She held several items in her hand: a greeting card that said, "Happy Birthday to the man I love," a small navy-blue gift bag and white wrapping tissue.

I was sure she was going to a birthday party for her husband. She placed the items on the countertop, then laid her oversized purse down as if to create a barrier between her stuff and mine.

The teenaged clerk scanned each item without much thought; she had obviously worked there for a while. The total was $5.97. The lady took a credit card out of her wallet. The clerk pointed to the machine on the counter and said, "Swipe towards me, we don't have a chip reader yet."

The cash machine spit out the receipt and the clerk tore it off, grabbed a pen and passed it to the lady saying, "Sign at the bottom." The tip of the pin slightly grazed the front of the purse.

Without warning, the lady grabbed the purse off the countertop startling both me and the clerk. She pushed it towards the clerk, her face filled with anger. "Look what you did!" she yelled, "Do you know what this purse cost? That ink mark better come out or you'll be replacing it!"

The young clerk froze, not knowing what to say at first then, "It was an accident. I don't see a mark." The lady slammed the purse down on the counter. "I see a mark and it better come out! This purse costs over $5,000! It's a real Louis Vuitton!"

It was then I realized she wasn't a young girl. I had only seen her from behind but as she berated the clerk, I could see her whole face. She was in her late forties maybe even early fifties. The lines around her eyes were deep and you could see where the make-up ended on her jaw line and her neck began.

She looked like a woman who had spent too much time in the sun or a tanning booth. Her lipstick was bright red, a colour that was much too young for her to wear. It was then I noticed her shoes. They were the black, plastic $19.97 pumps from Walmart. I know because I have the same ones.

I thought to myself, "Why would someone carrying a $5,000 purse wear cheap shoes from Walmart?

The clerk quickly bagged the lady's items. "I want the manager's name and phone number," she demanded. The clerk wrote the information on a piece of paper and handed it to her. The lady grabbed it from her fingers and put it in her pocket. She left the store with the Louis Vuitton over her shoulder and the Dollar Store bag in her hand. The clerk's face was red, sweat ran off her brow and she wiped it with her arm. She was shaking and tried to smile at me while saying, "Did you find everything you were looking for?" I nodded yes and her hands shook as she picked up each item to scan it.

After leaving the store I stopped at the food court for a coffee and to check my email. It wasn't until I sat down and opened my coffee that I realized Mrs. Louis Vuitton was sitting at the table next to me. She sat on the opposite side than I did. We were face to face. She was on her cell phone and didn't look at me. I only had a few emails, mostly items to delete, so I put the phone down and began my favourite sport of people watching.

My eyes kept wandering back to the overly dressed Mrs. Vuitton. Why hadn't she gone to her party? She put the blue gift bag on the table and took a small box out of her expensive purse. I recognized the name of the jewelry store on the front. She opened it and arranged the cufflinks so the birthday boy would see the monogrammed initial as soon as he opened the box. She put the box in the gift bag, then took out the wrapping tissue and arranged it like a handkerchief poking out of the bag. She took out the birthday card and opened it up. She searched through her expensive purse but couldn't find a pen. She finally noticed me sitting across from her and with a smile asked, "Do you have a pen I could borrow?" I lifted my blue Coach purse from the seat next to me. "Sure," I took out my cheap plastic pen and handed it to her. She wrote, "Love," then her name. She put the card in its envelope and placed it in the bag. She picked up her cell phone and continued to make calls. My pen was still in her hand.

It was then I noticed what Mrs. Vuitton was doing.

She had her ATM card out of her wallet; she was calling the number on the back. I could tell she got the recording to type in her card number and password because I've made that call from a mall many a time myself. She followed the instructions and continued pressing buttons. I knew she was checking the totals in her saving and chequing accounts.

She began biting her lower lip and hung up the phone. She took out the credit card she had used at the dollar store and called the number on the back. She entered the card number and continued to press numbers, checking the balance on her credit card. Then hung up. She took out a second credit card and did the same thing. The anxious look on her face told me she was at her limit. It was then I noticed she wasn't wearing a wedding ring.

As soon as she laid the phone back on the table it rang. She picked it up, "Hello. Oh, I see." She was oblivious to me and spoke like I couldn't hear her.

"Your children get the flu a lot lately. I have your birthday gift with me. I was looking forward to giving it to you."

There was a pause as she listened to the caller, "I know you told me no presents, but she won't notice this gift, I promise."

I realized the man on the other end, the birthday boy she was waiting for, was married. "Okay, I understand. Will I get to see you over the weekend?" The look on her face during the pause told me she wouldn't see him then either. She hung up the phone.

She picked up her Louis Vuitton purse that had been sitting on the chair next to her and placed it on the table. She put her cell phone inside. It was then I noticed it! Her "Louis Vuitton" was a "Louie Vuition!" It was spelled wrong. It was a fake! The purse cost no more than $35 at a Florida flea market. She had berated a teenage clerk at the Dollar Store over a cheap rip-off purse! She stood up, picked up her present and the cheap purse. She realized she still had my pen in her hand. "Thanks," she lied as she passed me the pen. She noticed my Coach purse on the table. "Nice purse," she smiled, "I love quality." She turned her back to me and walked away. Her cheap Walmart pumps clicked on the floor tile, her fake Louie over her shoulder, and her plans for the night squashed.

"Quality," I thought. It takes a small person to berate a teenager over accidentally marking a fake purse. A smaller person still to interfere with a marriage. Would she ever call the store manager? I doubt it. I watched her leave through the mall's doors. I picked up my authentic Coach purse. This woman didn't know the first thing about quality.

SPRING CLEANING IN AUGUST

I realize I am a little late for spring cleaning. It is August. I wish I could just shove the whole house into the dishwasher and be done with it.

I like doing housework. I always did. In BC (Before Children) I'd clean the house from top to bottom in four hours, only stopping for a can of Pepsi and a Du Maurier Light. Remember smoking? Back when we took fifteen-minute breaks every hour or so to have our smoke. Then we quit smoking and had no reason to take a break.

I am nocturnal, too. I like starting my cleaning around 10 PM and going till about 2 or 3 AM. That's why my kids sleep better if there is a vacuum going.

Then babies came along. We sold our small compact, easy-to-clean, one-bathroom house and bought a much bigger three-bathroom house. Three toilets to clean! What the hell was I thinking?

Anyway, I began my spring cleaning in August by shining up the front windows. Taking off the tape left from Halloween decorations and taking down the Christmas wreath.... Christmas wreath! How the hell did that slip by me? Half of me wants to leave it up and get an early start on next year. The other half says you've tortured the neighbours enough, take it down.

Next room was my tween-aged daughter's. Now, normally I make her clean her own room but every now and then I do go through it like the Tasmanian Devil just so the fire department doesn't condemn the house. I open the door and the smell of hairspray and nail polish is enough to take you off your feet. I believe that's why she acts like a zombie and her pupils are slightly dilated in the mornings.

I push my way through the shopping bags on the floor, clothes thrown all over the room, and try to open the curtain to let some light in. I can only assume this is what a crack house looks like on the inside. There's no way I can do this on my own.

A thought crosses my mind! Maybe I should call the insurance company and tell them our house was broken into! I'll say, "They didn't steal anything, they just ransacked the place." Maybe they'll send a cleaning crew. Then reason kicks in and I realize it's not worth jail-time.

Jail-time: lying in bed all day, having someone else cook and clean for you while I finish my university degree in peace. Universities should use that as a recruiting strategy. "Where did you finish your degree? In jail. Paid for by the government." The fumes are getting to me, too. I have to get out of here.

Son's room is like a museum. He never moves anything in his room because he lives in the basement playing video games. There's only a layer of dust. The cat jumps up on his dresser and walks across. I notice his tail is leaving a trail of clean. Maybe I should tie a dust cloth to his tail, and he can take care of the room. It's not worth the scratches.

I close the door; it will be another week or two before you can write your name in the dust. It's not an "Urgent" clean.

Our bedroom is cleanish. I do dust once a week and run the Swiffer over the hardwood floor. It only takes fifteen minutes. I get to hubby's side of the bed. Socks on the floor. Socks on the floor!!!

We've been living in this house for twelve years and he still can't figure out what the wicker laundry basket in the bedroom is for. I can't tell you how many times I've shown him how to take the cover off and put the damn socks inside. He says, "I leave them on the floor in case there's an emergency in the middle of the night. That way I know where they are."

What emergency? If someone breaks in while we're asleep, hubby will jump out of bed, pull on his socks and confront the thief! When he slides across the hardwood in only his underwear and socks, the poor crook will think he's being confronted by Tom Cruise and run like Katie Holmes.

Maybe he has a point there.

I tried having a house cleaner. I gave up. I spent the whole day before cleaning because I didn't want this stranger to think we were dirty.

The older I get the less I care how the house looks. I have never actually had anyone come in my house and notice the scuffed floors or try to write their name in the dust on my dresser.

Now that I am in my fifties, spring cleaning to me means sitting on my back patio sipping tea and brushing the pollen off my jeans.

Oh well, at least the Christmas wreath is down. The neighbours will be happy now.

OBSERVATIONS IN THE MALL: THE OLD LADY AND THE SEA

People watching is my favourite sport.

I love sitting in a public place watching people go by.

Guessing at what they do. Who they are. What their lives are like. It can entertain me for hours.

It was on one of my recent outings I noticed her. She sat alone in the shopping mall food court, drinking her tea from a paper coffee cup. I knew it was tea because of her age. She was in her late seventies or early eighties. That age range came to mind because she had an uncanny resemblance to my mother.

Her grey hair was short with the type of curls that could only come from rollers and setting lotion. Her black raincoat was open, revealing a white T-shirt with a floral design around the neck. Her polyester blue pants had a permanent crease in the legs and her sneakers, which I am sure she had chosen for comfort, had seen better days.

She sipped her tea and stared blankly ahead. Not noticing anyone around her. Just deep in thought. It was noon. If this were my mother, she would have wanted a sandwich or soup with her tea. Maybe she had eaten already.

I wondered if she was waiting for someone. A granddaughter maybe who had worn her out from shopping.

Now she was relaxing with her tea. Catching her second breath.

I had to go. I was meeting a friend for the 12:30 movie and I hadn't bought my ticket yet. I left the food court and the lady behind, hoping I hadn't left it too late to get a ticket.

When I arrived at the theatre my friend was waiting with two tickets in hand, predicting I had procrastinated.

It was after two by the time we left the theatre. We decided to shop for an hour before going home. We walked past the stores on the second level of the mall and my friend suggested we go downstairs. We passed the food court on the way to the escalator. I remembered the older lady. She wasn't at the table. I was just about to jump on the next revolving step on the escalator when I noticed she had moved. She was now sitting at the other end of the food court. "How odd," I thought. "She's still here."

We shopped for less than an hour and my back was killing me. My friend was parked in the underground parking lot and I was parked in the lot outside the food court. We parted ways and I continued up the escalator to the food court. I looked around but the lady was gone.

I knew before I hit the cold air, I had better use the washroom or it would be a painful ride home. There were washrooms off the food court, and I decided to make a detour. When I was washing my hands, I looked in the mirror and realized that the lady standing two sinks down from me was the same older lady I noticed earlier. She was trying to keep the water running but it was an automatic faucet that shut off after a few seconds to conserve water.

She noticed me staring this time. "I can't get this water to turn hot," she told me. "I don't think it gets hot. I think they just give you enough time to wash your hands, then it turns off automatically," I informed her.

As I dried my hands in the air dryer, she went back to trying to run the water. I watched her in the mirror. She glanced toward me and, seeing my back was to her, she took a clear plastic sandwich bag filled with tea bags out of her raincoat pocket. Then she took her paper coffee cup out of the other pocket. She took out a tea bag and placed it in the cup, then filled it with cool water. She put the brown plastic cover over the top of the cup, picked it up and left the washroom.

I gave her a few seconds then walked out behind her. She walked over to a table, sat down, and began to drink her tea. She didn't speak to anyone. She just stared, deep in thought as before.

My cell phone rang. "Don't forget I need white nylons for my dance concert," my daughter reminded me. White nylons. Where do I find them? There was a drug store just off the food court. I went in search of white nylons. Twenty-five minutes later, I was ready to leave the mall. I walked through the food court expecting to see the older lady sitting at the table, but she was gone. The table was clean.

As I left through the food court doors, I caught a glimpse of her getting on a bus. I walked to my car and never saw her again. Thoughts of her consumed me on the drive home.

Why would an elderly woman spend almost four hours sitting in a food court? Who knows how long she was there before I spotted her. Why did she have her own tea bags in her pocket? Who was she? Her wrinkled face told me she had worked hard all her life and probably raised a family.

Did they know she was here all afternoon? Did they care?

Is she one of the forgotten elderly? The ones who sit at the mall all day because they can't afford to heat their houses. Or one of the boarding house residents who are not allowed to stay home during the day and have to find a place to go. The mall would be a safe place for these people. Surely no security guard would ask an elderly woman to move along and stop loitering.

Then it hit me.

The table was clean! The cup was gone. Did she take the cup with her?

I'll look for her the next time I am at the mall.

Maybe I'll be so bold as to ask her if I can sit with her.

I'll tell her that she reminds me of my own mother.

I'll ask if I can buy her a cup of tea.

Supermodels can't really fly

While flipping through my favourite fashion magazine, I noticed some weird trends:

1. Someone shot all the supermodels with a Taser gun and knocked them out
2. Women who model purses never look inside them
3. Models have horrible posture
4. Madonna has bad cramps
5. Why do women have to be naked to sell jewelry?
6. Fashion has just gotten silly

Like, I am an 80's girl. I grew up with supermodels who were beautiful… Christie Brinkley, Cindy Crawford, Elle Macpherson. All stunning, and glowy and bright.

My latest issue of Vogue features models that look strung out, passed out, and just out! Half the time I don't know what they are selling.

There is an advertisement of a model laying across the bed. The ad is for a purse, but when was the last time you got in bed with your purse? I mean I love my purses as much as the next gal and I often dream of them when I am in bed, but take one to bed? I don't think so. It's just not realistic. Why does she look passed out? I just want to shake her and say, "Don't fall asleep with that much makeup on, you'll get zits."

Why don't models ever look in the purse? If you're going to sell me a purse show me how much junk it can hold. I want to see a model looking through the purse with her iPhone in her mouth, her makeup bag under her arm, her wallet in one hand while she is looking for her keys with the other but pulls out the TV remote instead. Now I would buy that purse!

Then there are the Madonna Versace ads. Now like I said, I am an 80's girl and I loved Madonna all through the whole crucifix phase, the wearing her bras on the outside, the freedom of expression, but there's something off about these pictures.

Is the purse too heavy? Is her back out from dancing? Is she taking a quick fart break in between photos? Is it period cramps? Is she tired? What's up? I don't get it. If I were wearing a Versace dress and carrying a Versace purse, I would be standing proud with that thing slung over my shoulder like a boss. But not a Hugo Boss.

What was going through the photographer's head? "Madonna, bend over like you're trying to fart through two pairs of Spanx, and we will put a concrete block in the purse so your arms will look even more toned when you try to pick it up. Now work it, Material Girl. Work that gas out."

I think the look on Madonna's face says it all. "I'll

crack your head with the cheeks of my ass if you say that one more time, bitch." I think Madonna would say that. I would if I had her arms. I love Madonna.

Then there's the posture thing. When did slouching become a model pose?

The model on another page looks scary thin, which is probably why it looks like she can barely hold the purse. But her back is so rounded she looks like she should be in a brace.

I can hear the Nuns at Our Lady of Mercy School in my head saying, "You're going to end up looking like the Hunchback of Notre Dame if you don't straighten up." Then I would snap to attention and straighten my spine.

I guess this model wasn't raised Catholic.

It took me a while to figure out the models on another page were selling shoes and accessories.

I just don't know why they have to be naked to do it.

Wouldn't the jewelry look better with clothes?

When I buy jewelry, I like to see how it looks with what I am wearing or plan on wearing. Maybe I am doing it wrong.

The next time I am in a jewelry store I am going to take my top off and try on a necklace, then ask the salesperson how I look. If they say, "Stunning! Model like!" Then I am going to buy it. If they call the cops, they won't make a sale from me. I'll let you know if it works.

I noticed a dress advertised as Haute Couture. Maybe I am missing something. Maybe art is in the eye of the beholder, but to me the model looks like she ran through a glass wall, made a dress from the broken pieces, and may have hurt herself badly because she is obviously bleeding to death.

Where would you wear this? I imagine myself walking into a huge ballroom and a waiter coming over with soda water and a napkin to help take the bloodstain out of my dress. Or the police showing up questioning me about where my husband is. Or my mother coming back from the dead to ask, "You're not really going to wear that, are you?"

Am I missing something? This dress is plain silly to me.

Is it a case of the Emperor's New Clothes?

I know the 80s had its faults, but it also had the glamour.

You just don't see glamour in fashion anymore. I think the grunge years did it in and it just never recovered.

Having said that, I won't be cancelling my subscription to Vogue anytime soon either. I've loved that magazine all through the years. I even turned a blind eye when they put a Kardashian on the cover.

Maybe I have fallen out of fashion's target market.

Maybe my Carrie Bradshaw days ended with the TV series.

Maybe I am too old to understand it anymore.

Maybe Madonna is slouched over because the weight of being a fashion icon is too much for her to carry?

I am going to have to sleep on it. I am going to take my favourite purse to bed with me tonight and see if I am missing something, and my black stilettos.

No, maybe not the stilettos, that would only get hubby excited… but it would give me more time to think about my purse collection.

THERE BUT FOR THE GRACE OF GOD GO I

My daughter went to a music summer camp in July and their final performance was held at an Irish pub and restaurant downtown. It's a wonderful program that allows young people a chance to play in a live band and perform in front of a crowd.

My husband, son and I couldn't wait to see our daughter perform with a live band in a pub setting. The final performance was held on a Friday afternoon. We decided to meet there for lunch first to ensure we found a parking space and made the show on time.

The kids did an awesome job performing and the food was fabulous. While we were eating, I couldn't help but notice an elderly lady sitting alone at the table across from us drinking a beer.

This lady was probably in her seventies, with blond hair piled on top of her head. Her front teeth were missing, and she was dressed more like a teenager than a senior. The lines on her face were a telltale sign that she had lived a hard life and her overall appearance told you that she suffered from mental illness. She is a regular character in the downtown area.

By the time the waitress brought us our food the pub was filled with families of the children attending the camp.

Before too long there wasn't an empty table in the club and the only empty chair was the one on the opposite end of the table this elderly woman sat at.

I couldn't stop watching her out of the corner of my eye. The loneliness in her face was hard to ignore. Maybe it was the passing of my mother that year that made me notice this woman.

My mother had a soft spot for women who lived hard lives because she knew firsthand how hard life could be. She would have approached this lady and said hello and asked if she was okay.

When I was growing up, I would get embarrassed when my mother approached someone like this lady and would ask, "Why do you have to talk to every hard luck story we pass?" She would always answer with, "There but for the grace of God go I."

I noticed she took some coins out of her pocket and counted a few loonies and toonies, then put them away again. The waitress brought an order of fish and chips and laid it on the table in front of her and, in no time, she cleaned her plate.

She took out her change again and counted it. It didn't look like she had enough to pay for her meal and beer.

By that time, the waitress had brought our bill and told us we could pay at the counter when we were ready. I took the bill from my husband's hand and said, "My treat," and met our waitress at the counter. I pointed out the lady sitting alone and asked the waitress to put her food on our bill. She said, "You don't have to do that." "Yes, I do," I told her, "go ahead and put it on my bill."

"No," she said, "you don't have to do that because she eats here for free."

"Really?"

"Yes, the owner lets her eat for free." I was dumbfounded. I looked back at this lady sitting alone at the table and thought not many restaurants would even let her sit inside with their paying customers but here, at this Irish pub, not only is she welcome, but she also eats for free!

I could only think that the owner, like my mother, knew what hard times were like. He must also look at this lady and think, "There but for the grace of God go I."

I went back to my table. The lady was standing and putting her coat back on. She reached into her pocket and took out her change. She picked out a toonie and laid it on the table, then quietly walked out.

The families of the children performing were erupting in applause as a song ended. Families all there to support their children. I watched the blond-haired lady walk down Water Street, wondering if she had family.

My Mother would look at a lady like that and say, "Somebody did something to her that made her life turn out like that. No one chooses to be that way."

I watched her disappear into a crowd of tourists and thought to myself, "There but for the grace of God go I."

DON'T TALK TO YOUR TEENAGED DAUGHTER LIKE I DO, IT DOESN'T WORK!

I can't remember the last time my teenaged daughter asked for advice. Advice on anything! I think I've been replaced by Google.

I think back on all the good advice my mother shared with me and now I have a dory-load of good advice to share.

Like, don't sit on the seat in a public washroom, and if you do have to sit, put toilet paper down first. Then hold the fork of your underwear out with one hand while you're using it, so your underwear doesn't touch the toilet.

This info must be shared.

Not everyone knows to hold the fork of their underwear away from the bowl!

I Googled "How to talk to your teenage daughter" and came up with some great tips.

Like:

Start Talking to Your Daughter Early.

Great tip. I sat on her bed at 6:30 AM and started telling her about my day ahead. She wasn't open to it at all. She literally kicked me off the bed and threw me out of her room and I am not that light, so it was a huge chore for her to get me off the floor. Those dance lessons are really paying off.

Be Open When You Talk with Your Daughter.

I started with, "I was twenty-one the first time I had sex. How old were you?" She ran away from me so fast the salesgirl at the store we were in thought she was a shoplifter and called security to chase her. They found her in the parking lot, hiding behind a van, but I told them she was just trying to get away from me.

Find the Balance Between Friend and Mother.

I thought this one was going to be easy. I showed up at her school dance in my Tina Turner black leather mini skirt and matching boob-tube, snuck up behind her and said, "Let's ask those two cuties over there to dance." She called Child Protective Services on herself and asked if any foster homes were available.

Be Detailed in Talks with Your Daughter.

I started the conversation with, "We haven't discussed yeast infections yet, have we?" I followed it up with detailed pictures that we could discuss but she spent so much time with her head in the toilet, throwing up, I gave up on the conversation.

Use Everyday Media to Trigger Conversations with Your Daughter.

I sincerely asked, "Do you think Kim's ass really broke the internet? Because I think those screaming goats did a better job." Now she has installed a lock on the inside of her bedroom door and a cat door so her father can slide food in.

In the end, I don't think mothers or daughters should trust Google to help them communicate or for advice.

Finally, God intercepted. She yelled out "Mom, I think I have a fever." I ran upstairs, into the bathroom, grabbed the thermometer (not the rectal one), Vicks VapoRub, Tylenol Cold and the Halls cough drops.

She allowed me to take care of her for a whole twenty minutes before kicking me out of the room. I was in heaven.

I was needed.

Google may be good, but it can't comfort a sick child... or use a rectal thermometer with love.

REMEMBER THAT GIRL WE BULLIED IN 1998, MONICA LEWINSKY? HAVE YOU APOLOGIZED TO HER YET?

1998 seems like a hundred years ago. I was in my early thirties and working in radio when the story of the Monica Lewinsky affair with Bill Clinton broke. We never saw the likes of it before. It was the start of a cultural change: cyber-bullying and online harassment at its worst.

I just watched her Ted Talk and I highly recommend you do, too.

It's titled, "The Price of Shame." How fitting. She was a twenty-two-year-old intern who fell in love with her handsome, powerful, and charismatic boss, The President of the United States. Her naïve outlook on love had devastating consequences for her.

Twenty-two years old! My God, my son is twenty. I live in fear of one of my children becoming the victim of online shaming.

I can only imagine what her parents went through. In the Ted Talk she reveals her mother made her shower with the door open to make sure she did not kill herself. There are almost forty rap songs that reference her affair with Clinton. Few mention Clinton.

When people hear the name "Monica Lewinsky" they will always think "blow job." When they hear the name "Bill Clinton" they will always think "President of the

United States." How fair is that?

She will always wear the Scarlet Letter and her name will be followed by slut, whore, bimbo, tart or "That woman."

She lists them off in her Ted Talk. It made me feel ashamed.

He will always be "Mr. President." She was twenty-two. He took advantage of her.

She refers to herself as "Patient Zero" of cyberbullying. When the story broke in 1998 it was the first time a major news story played out online as well as in the traditional media. People around the world, all new to the internet, turned into an angry mob and Monica Lewinsky became a hated and hunted woman.

At twenty-two she became a global whore. Billed as if she was the first woman to have sex with her boss. He was still "Mr. President." Wait! Oh, that's right: "He did not have sex with that woman!"

That woman! At twenty-two she became "that woman."

At twenty-two she began to live a life of public, worldwide humiliation. Her life stopped. The possibilities that her future held, ended. At twenty-two she no longer had a future because she had sex with her boss.

What frustrates me the most is that I took part in it. You did too. We all told the Monica Lewinsky jokes. We listened to them. We still think "blow job" instead of "victim" when we hear her name. Over time, we became numb to these jokes because she wasn't a real person to us. We didn't think about a twenty-two-year-old on suicide watch. We didn't think about her mother crying every night and her father's helplessness as he watched his little girl's life destroyed over a sex act.

We could recognize her face because we saw it every day on the internet or in the media. We didn't know she had a soul. We didn't think about her feelings. We didn't have empathy or sympathy for her.

We almost humiliated this girl to death.

Eighteen years later public shaming has become an industry. Celebrities and reality stars traffic in it. But she was different. She didn't release a sex tape. She didn't want to be famous for a sex act. She was twenty-two. I fill up just thinking about her and what she went through.

Hillary Clinton wants to be President now, at the time I write this. I cannot find anything online that says that she met with Monica Lewinsky and forgave her for her role in the affair.

Should she? Should the wife forgive the mistress? I think it depends. How long is she going to continue to nail this poor girl to the cross?

Bill Clinton has never apologized to her. He took advantage of a twenty-two-year girl. He abused his power. He was President. To put it in perspective, four years earlier Monica was in high school.

At twenty-two I made mistakes. Lots of them. That's what twenty-two-year-olds do. They make mistakes and they learn from them. She didn't commit a crime. She fell in love, at twenty-two, with a handsome, powerful, charismatic man. Her boss.

I apologize.

I am sorry, Monica, for reading those jokes, repeating them, and sharing them. I had no idea you were a real person. I got caught up in a public slut shaming mob and I didn't know we almost drove you to your death.

Monica is now an advocate for people who are victims of cyber-bullying and online harassment. Who better than her? She is no longer a "victim" but a "survivor."

How do we change it?

In her Ted Talk, Monica says stop reading online shaming and humiliation. Every time you click on an online shaming story about a celebrity, the provider of that content makes money. The more clicks, the more money. This is an industry. She says, "Public shaming as a blood sport has to stop" and she is right.

We all need to build a circle of protection around this lady.

She has suffered enough. The next time I hear Monica Lewinsky's name said in a derogatory way I will respond with, "Did you know she was twenty-two? Do you know she was a victim? Do you know she is human?"

I will not click on public shaming stories about celebrities or participate in internet mobs that destroy lives.

Ask yourself, "What if this was my daughter? How would I feel?"

She is right. Public shaming as a blood sport must stop.

It stops with you.

THE BEST WAY TO LOSE WEIGHT... DOG!

The best way to lose weight is... dog! No, you don't EAT it, you WALK it (that's WALK not WOK). It's called the "Dog Diet."

Over the years, I have tried every diet known to woman.

From famous brand names to the cabbage soup diet. They all work for a week, then I just gain it all back once the diet is over.

There are so many crazy diets on the market if you Google weight loss. For example, the "Cotton Ball" diet. Yes, you eat cotton balls to fill you up. It's a real thing, but no thanks, I have enough stuffing; that's why I am Googling weight loss.

Or how about the thirty-day cleanse where you don't digest anything for thirty days except juice and water. A better name would be Anorexia 101: an introduction to eating disorders.

I just want to fit comfortably into my size ten jeans. I don't want a role on the Hunger Games. I like food. Food is my friend. Don't tell me to stay away from my friend.

When I open the door to my closet, I start to hear Whitney Houston's song "I am Every Woman" because I have been every woman over the years. My jeans start at a size eight and go up to a twelve, and I wear them all depending on the month, my mood, whether I am retaining water, pregnant, bitchy, menstruating, ovulating, going through the change, happy, sad, or somewhere in between.

Recently I joined a gym and hired a personal trainer. It seemed like a good idea at the time. This buff twenty-something-year-old and I sat down and went through my wish list: I want to be toned not muscular. I want to look good in a bathing suit not compete in a weightlifting competition. I want my stomach tight and my arms toned. I told him, "When I am wearing a T-shirt and I wave at someone I don't want the turkey skin under my arm waving twice as fast as my hand. You know what I mean?" He stared at me blankly. I think he understood.

I made it through two of six sessions with him. During the second session he showed me how to do a Turkish sit-up (you'll have to Google it). You lay on the mat with a ten-pound weight in your left hand, then you use your right hand to arch your body off the mat and put the ten-pound weight in the air over your head. I did give it shot. I got to three and sat down.

"I don't like this," I told him. He assures me this was the best way to get my core in shape. I reminded him about my back surgery and limitations, and I could tell he was getting frustrated with me. I finally said, "Look, I have about thirty years on you. I have given birth twice and I have made peace with the fact that my hips are never going back to where they were twenty years ago. I am going through a change of life and could start to cry at any moment so don't pressure me, and I would much rather be going through McDonald's drive-thru right now than doing Turkish sit-ups with you."

He looked at me like he knew he was getting dumped.

I felt obliged to say, "It's not you, it's me. I have a fear of commitment when it comes to gym memberships; that's why I only bought the month."

He started in on the "Don't give up on me" speech but my mind was made up when I hit the mat on the third try. "It's over. You're too young for me. Isn't there a personal trainer who is in their fifties or sixties that I could work with?"

He assured me he would design a plan just for me and that age didn't matter. Like, what am I, a gym cougar?

I could feel the muscle in my neck going into a spasm. "Ya know what? This is just not working for me." I cancelled my membership on the way out, went to McDonalds and got a low-calorie Egg McMuffin and ate it in the car. According to my last diet plan it's only two points so I am good with that.

I have realized that the only six pack I am going to have is in my fridge.

I went home and threw my gym gear back in the closet.

Minnie, my dog and BFF (Best Fury Friend), was whining to go out. I put her leash around her neck, put my earbuds in, and walked her around the block. It was a good thirty-five-minute walk and the "MyFitnessPal" App on my iPhone says it gave me back 273 calories (it allows me to have 1200 a day). The egg McMuffin was already gone.

I walked her again later that night and lost another 273 calories. After a week of walking Minnie twice a day, I lost three pounds and didn't change my eating at all. After three weeks I was down ten pounds and that was the only thing I did different. (I also drink three bottles of water a day anyway). As it turns out, Minnie was the best personal trainer I ever had.

She is also a great listener. I could talk to her about anything. She never lets my secrets out or talks about me behind my back. She agrees with everything I say and follows me all over the house. She doesn't judge me when we go through the McDonalds drive-thru and encourages me to have treats throughout the day.

It's the "dog diet." It's the latest celebrity craze, or at least that's what I am telling everyone one.

Who knew walking everyday could make you lose weight?

Crazy right?

THINGS YOU SHOULDN'T HAVE TO PAY FOR, LIKE PEEING

Remember when you had to pay a dime to pee in a store restroom? The urge would strike in the middle of Woolco, you would run through the aisles to the washroom at the back of the store only to find out you didn't have a dime to put in the door. I guess employees at Woolco got tired of cleaning the pee off the floor and decided to let you have this basic human right for free.

Smart choice, I think. There are some things you shouldn't make money off. Pee is one. Healthcare is another.

I remember one time when my daughter was about nine, she had the flu. It was getting worse by the hour. She was throwing up continuously and couldn't keep so much as a glass of water down. Her fever shot through the roof and I decided to take her to the Children's Hospital. I didn't take her to the hospital right away because there was a raging winter storm happening outside and I didn't want to drive when the roads were snow-covered and slippery.

I put her in her snowsuit, belted her in the middle seat of the minivan and made my way to the hospital slipping and sliding all the way.

When I drove into the parking lot there wasn't a space available. The lot was full. I had to park in the lot at the main hospital. By the time I found a spot, she was sound asleep. I lifted her ninety-pound body in my arms and made my way through the storm like I was walking through the Arctic tundra. The snow plough had made a four-foot-high wall of snow around the lot and I bravely scaled it without dropping my daughter.

By the time I got to the Emergency entrance I looked like a nomad that had been wandering the ice plains for years. I was exhausted and ready to pass out myself. After a four hour wait, we finally saw a doctor who confirmed she had pneumonia and needed antibiotics.

I bundled her back up and made the long trek back to the minivan only to find I had a parking ticket!

A parking ticket! Seriously! Police were warning drivers to stay off the roads, but meter maids made it to work!

Steam was coming out of my ears! In my rush to get my sick child through a storm to see a doctor I forgot to put money in the parking meter. I was furious. Why the hell should I have to pay this ticket? I wasn't shopping. I had a child with pneumonia. A ninety-pound child that I had carried through a snowstorm, sat in a waiting room for four hours with and then carried back to my van. I should have been given a frigging Olympic medal for the Mom triathlon! Not a parking ticket.

I tried to leave the parking lot, but the snow was about a foot deep around my van. On top of everything else, now I was stuck in the snow. I kept putting the van in drive and reverse till I finally rocked it out of the parking space. By this time my anger level was at an all-time high. I put the van in reverse and floored it. The van jumped out of its tracks and flew back a good two feet, hitting the parking meter. I got out to look. The pole was bent a little and the head of the meter slightly hung down in shame. I kicked it and said, "You deserved that you bastard!"

Why are there meters in hospital parking lots?

Another thing. What's up with the TV rentals? My eighty-five-year-old mother was in hospital for weeks. Her kidneys were failing. A valve in her heart was leaking and her body was dying. She loved her soap operas. It would kill her to die and not know what was happening on Days of Our Lives. She rented a TV with basic cable.

$11.50 a day plus tax! That's what they charged this dying senior on a fixed income! Who the hell is making money off my dying mother and her soap operas? Are you telling me the Department of Health can't negotiate a better deal than that?

Why can't they buy cable for the hospital and give it to patients for free? This is so wrong!

What happens to the people who can't afford to pay $11.50 a day? They just lay there in bed all day, staring out the window. They're forced to eat hospital food three times a day. Aren't they suffering enough? You're telling me the government can't afford free TV for the sick? How much can Wi-Fi for the hospital cost?

There's an old saying, "You judge a country by how it treats its most vulnerable, its poor, its sick, its weak."

There are some things you shouldn't have to pay for in life. A toilet to pee in. A parking space at the hospital when you have an emergency. A TV when you're dying. Basic human rights that shouldn't have to be written down because they are common sense.

If I have to pay an extra few cents in taxes to cover that, so be it. A dying woman should not have to miss her soap operas because she's broke. A nine-year-old girl with pneumonia shouldn't be given a parking ticket. A woman with a bladder problem shouldn't have to pee in her pants because she doesn't have a dime, and governments should not have to be shamed into doing the right thing.

THE GOLDWING AND THE CAT

Fall is in the air and hubby says it's time to put the Goldwing in storage for the winter. He is going to start winterizing the bike this week. It made me think back to a couple of years ago when I drove a minivan that I could never park properly.

Our house is on a corner lot. There is a one car driveway in the front of the house where the garage is, which is mine, and a two-car driveway on the side, which is for hubby's toys.

One Saturday I left with our daughter to go to her dance classes and hubby stayed home to winterize the Goldwing so he could store it for the winter.

After dancing for two hours and trying to recover from a birthday party sleep-over, my daughter was not in a good mood to say the least. She was cranky, tired, and simply hard to handle. By the time I got back home she was having a complete meltdown and looked like the Exorcist in the back seat. I was trying to back into the driveway while looking into my side-mirrors to make sure I was staying on the asphalt. At the same time, I was trying to keep an eye on Linda Blair in the back seat to make sure her head was not doing a complete 360.

Then I heard a "Bang!"

I looked in the rear-view mirror but could not see anything. I looked in the side-view mirrors and could not see anything. I was too far away from the garage door to hit it. I put the van in park and jumped out.

There, laying wounded on the driveway, was hubby's pride and joy, his only reason for living, his prized Goldwing. Lying on its side... softly crying.

I knew I was going to be killed. I had to think fast. I pulled the minivan out of the driveway and parked it on the street. I got the Exorcist out of the back and dragged her in the house kicking and screaming. I called out to hubby, but he did not answer. I ran upstairs looking for him. By the time I got to our bedroom I could hear him in the driveway cursing and swearing. I ran back downstairs and out to the driveway. Before I could say, "Sorry," he looked at me and said, "I am going to kill that cat!"

"The cat?" What did the cat have to do with anything? I thought to myself.

He saw the question marks in my eyes that were holding back the flood of tears that I was getting ready to spill while I begged for forgiveness.

"That God damn cat knocked over my bike. I went to the basement to get something and when I came back the cat was sitting on the bike. She must have jumped from the porch roof." He stood there scratching his head, looking from the porch roof to the bike.

"The cat! Yes, that damn cat," I agreed with him. I was a woman on death row and if I had to sell-out the cat then so be it.

"I've always hated that cat!"

"Help me pick it up," he asked. I did my wifely duty and helped him put the bike upright. The taillight was broken and there was a big black scratch from the asphalt.

"There's no damage at all," I lied. He was pissed. I tiptoed back into the house where I knew I would be safer with the Exorcist.

Now, hubby is a retired police officer and a damn good one at that. He spent many years at accident scenes and was considered an expert witness in a court room. It did not take long for his police gut feelings to kick in.

About twenty minutes later I had calmed the Exorcist down and let her have a nap. I was enjoying a cup of tea while watching TV when hubby came back into the house. He calmly sat in his armchair and said, "You know that cat is only about ten pounds."

Immediately my brain said, "Dead Woman Walking!" I had to think quickly. "Nooooo. She must be handy on thirty pounds. You should see what she eats. She looks like a seal with legs."

He quietly nodded his head and answered, "Even at thirty pounds, if she was propelled from a rocket launcher at a 1,000-pound motorcycle, she still wouldn't knock it over."

"It was probably one of those perfect storms." I was drowning here. "When the cat jumped from the roof and the wind was at a perfect speed and the bike was at the perfect angle. You know, like one of those freak accidents."

"Or," he said, "like when someone backs their minivan into the driveway without looking in the rear-view mirror to make sure there's nothing there first." Dead woman walking! Dead woman walking!

"Who would do that and not tell us?" I asked, shocked.

"Well maybe it was someone with my bike paint on their rear bumper," he answered. I knew he had me. My only hope was to throw myself on the mercy of the court and to turn it around and make him believe it was his fault.

"Well, you should not have parked it in my driveway. You know I cannot park on the best of days. This is your fault."

He calmly got up and said, "I am going to Canadian Tire to buy a tail-light for my bike. It is in the front driveway. Try not to kill it the next time you park the van." Then he left.

I watched him walk away thinking, this is a trap. He has booby-trapped the house to blow up when he gets to the bottom of the street. Or maybe he cut the brake-lines on my van. Or maybe cut off the heels on my favourite stilettos. There has to be retaliation for this.

I have been waiting two years. Still nothing. Whenever he mentions putting the bike away for the winter, I start sleeping with one eye open. I know it is coming.

Maybe revenge is best when it is served cold, but does it have to be moldy, too?

RETIREMENT: A TIME TO FIND OUT WHO YOU ARE NOW

Today was the first day I enjoyed retirement.

Which is weird because I retired two years ago. I brewed a pot of coffee, turned the TV on, and caught the beginning of a Tom Selleck movie. I curled up on the couch in my housecoat, curious to see if Tom solves the crime and gets the girl.

Here I was at 9:20 AM drinking hot coffee and watching a movie. Three cups of coffee later and close on eleven o'clock, Tom solved the crime and got the girl. I could see that coming. After all, I just retired from a career in policing. I used to be the Senior Communications Strategist with the Royal Canadian Mounted Police (RCMP).

Now I am a veteran. It feels funny even saying it.

After the movie I did a half an hour of yoga and a short meditation. Even now I have knots in my neck and back from years of stress that I cannot get rid of. I learned to meditate a few years ago to help me not kill people who irritated me. It must work because I am not incarcerated. I took a long shower and had a brief moment of madness because I shaved my whole leg – not just below the knee – and I am not even wearing a skirt today. By the time I got out of the shower it was almost one o'clock. I am trying to learn to relax but it was irritating me that I accomplished nothing today.

I do not know why I consider relaxing as "accomplishing nothing." I knew I had to get dressed. My daughter would be home from school shortly and I did not want her to find me still in my housecoat in the middle of the day. I dried my hair, put on some make up and got dressed. There I sat at 2:30 in the afternoon, legs shaved, hair done, make up on and nowhere to go.

How do you know when it is time to retire? I get asked that all the time by my old coworkers. The truth is... you just know. For me, I was sitting in a meeting when a supervisor made what I considered a bad decision about my Communications Unit. A few months earlier that would have enraged me. We would have battled over it for weeks.

But I just sat there taking notes, saying nothing, being silent. I went back to my office and my partner at the time asked, "What happened? You didn't say anything." I realized I did not say anything because I didn't care. I always said when the job was not fun anymore, I would retire. That day was this day. It was not fun anymore. There was no fight left in me. I was burned out. I knew it was time to take my ball and go home. I called HR and asked, "How do I retire?"

That last day, I walked out of headquarters conflicted. It felt like I was going through a bad divorce. A divorce I was not even sure I wanted. I felt like I loved the husband I was about to leave but I knew it was time to let him go. I had a knot in my stomach thinking, what if I want to go back? Would he take me back? Will he replace me as soon as I leave? Because I thought I could never be replaced.

Eventually they did post my job and replaced me. I felt disappointed because I really thought the RCMP would close without me. Eventually the husband I was not sure I wanted to divorce replaced me with someone half my age, more educated and bilingual. Someone who probably shaves her whole leg every day.

I ran at freedom like an escaped convict. I felt the need to fill every moment of my day with stuff to do. First thing I did was book a trip with the husband I had not divorced. We went to Florida and took a wonderful cruise through the Caribbean. While my husband whined about returning to work, I had no idea what I was returning to. A few weeks later I took my daughter to Toronto to see her favourite boy band in concert. It was so different to spend time alone with her without my BlackBerry constantly ringing. Even now I can still feel the vibration of the BlackBerry on my left hip and I reach to answer it.

A week after I retired, I bought a gym membership and hired a personal trainer. He was a twenty-two-year-old university student who kept barking orders at me and shouting, "push yourself." By day five I fired him. I was honest when I said, "It's not you. It's me." I explained, "You're twenty-two. I am fifty. Pushing myself means putting on a pair of Spanx and control top pantyhose." It was too much too soon.

Then one day it happened... the meltdown. While watching the evening news a story about the RCMP came on. "Why aren't we reacting?" I shouted at the TV. We should have someone out in front of this with media lines to give our side of the story. I was enraged and I immediately reached for my BlackBerry, preparing to go into crisis communication mode. But there was no BlackBerry.

The next morning, I went into headquarters for a veterans meeting. I ran into my old partner and tried to have a conversation about the news the night before. I told him he needed to pull out my old media lines. I explained, "You need to do this! You need to do that!" He stood there politely listening to me. Then he dropped the bomb... "You know I can't discuss that with you." I realized I had put him in an awkward situation. He could not discuss a police operation with a civilian. I know that. We both walked away. It was then I realized I was on the outside now. The divorce was final. I was just served my papers.

I had to find something to do with myself. I cannot handle "alone time." I had been writing a blog called "I am Funny Like That" for a few years and decided I would focus on it more.

I figured there must be somebody who wanted free communication advice. I had always been a volunteer in our church. Now I dove in. I wrote a communication strategy to bring people back to church. I targeted minority groups, especially the long-neglected LGBT community. I mean, if I can spin police stories then of course I could bring families in by the droves on Sunday morning. Laugh if you want but it worked to the point that the Bishop said we were getting too much publicity and to tone it down.

I started volunteering with my children's Air Cadet Squadron and took on the Duke of Edinburgh program. I now have nineteen cadets in various levels, and I spend my weekends hiking the East Coast trail with them. At the same time, I volunteer as communications director for another charity. I spent the last two years creating communication strategies around fundraising and I was extremely successful. I am immensely proud of everything I have accomplished since I retired. The problem is, I created a full-time job for myself.

Just recently, after a gruelling fundraising effort, I asked myself, "Why did I retire?" If I want to work full-time, I should have stayed in the RCMP. I realized I had to retire from my retirement. I need to learn how to relax. I need to learn how to retire.

The best advice I received was from a fellow veteran. He told me retirement gives you a lot of time to think. He advised that one day I will be doing some menial task around the house and suddenly, I will remember something that happened ten or fifteen years ago. A meeting where I overreacted. A partner that I snapped at. Something I would like to do over again. He advised, "Then you will beat yourself up for the rest of the day thinking 'Why did I say that?' 'Why didn't I do this?'" He advised me to let it go, think about something else, and he was right. It is like your brain downloads everything you went through at random times. I am glad he told me that because it really does happen, and you need to be prepared for memories that can keep you up all night.

I joined a line dancing group (don't laugh, it is fun) because I was warned to stay social. I went out for lunch with this group of women. One of the ladies was having a "crisis" because the oven in her stove was broken. She went on and on about the oven. I sat there staring at her. I did not know how to react to a broken oven. I was thinking, "A year ago I was giving media advice on major crime investigations, reading situation reports on horrific acts of child abuse, and the month before I retired three of our members were murdered in Moncton."

I wanted to say something, but I couldn't. I could not relate to this woman's "crisis". She was too normal. I sat there, smiled, and pretended I could relate to her "crisis", knowing I needed to redefine "crisis" now.

I decided to stick to the friends I already had and focus on my family. I started baking cookies in the afternoon so when my daughter came home from school, she would have an afternoon snack with me. Maybe we could talk and get to know each other. It worked. After a while I found she was a nice person. It took retirement for me to realize that I raised the daughter I always wanted. I had no idea how funny, intelligent, thoughtful, and amazing my daughter had become.

I had to re-introduce myself to my husband. He must have thought, "Who is this woman who bakes cookies and shaves her full leg?" We had been married for twenty years and I had no idea who he was now. I was just too busy raising kids, having a full-time career, and being that woman who had it all. We must have liked each other at some point, we had two children together! For years, I passed him in the hallway in the mornings. I would see him briefly in the evening while I was running to dance with our daughter, and he was running to cadets with our son. One night I sat on the couch, watching him furiously answer emails on his BlackBerry. I think it was the first time I really looked at him in years. He was quite handsome. I do not know why that surprised me. He was good looking when I married him twenty years ago! I realized then; it took retirement to make me fall in love with the man I had already been in love with for twenty years.

Today, I retired from my retirement. I have given up most of my charity work, except for the Air Cadet's Duke of Edinburgh program. I enjoy working with teens. I find they breathe life back in me and it is truly rewarding to see them achieve their goals in this program. I have learned to say, "No," I am not available to others, and I try not to feel bad about that.

My next quest is to find a balance between my family, my volunteerism, and discovering who I am now. All in all, retirement is great. It just takes time to let go of your old life and find a new one. There is a normal grieving process.

I have learned that enjoying retirement means it is not a waste of time to cuddle with Tom Selleck in the morning and have a fully shaved leg in the afternoon. It is time well spent.

Some advice for those about to retire, stay away from personal trainers. After all, you just retired from a career where someone barks orders at you. Buy a good pair of Spanx instead.

THE SECRET TO A GOOD MARRIAGE IS A GOOD POT-ROAST

A happy marriage is easy to achieve if you know what you are doing. I discovered early in mine that a pot-roast can greatly improve your marital bliss.

Hubby never wants anything fancy. His idea of spice is salt and pepper. He is a meat and potato kind of guy. We take turns cooking. He BBQ's like a pro and I do my cooking in the kitchen.

First thing every morning for over twenty years he has asked, "What's for supper?" Then he will call me at some point during the day, make small-talk and slip in, "What's for supper?" He will call when he leaves the office to ask how my day was and ask nonchalantly, "What's for supper?"

About ten years into the marriage I started to notice a pattern. In the morning when he asked, "What's for supper?" if I told him, "Spaghetti," he would be in a bad mood.

He would call during the day and ask, "What's for supper?" and I'd repeat, "Spaghetti," and he would go on about what a bad day he had.

Then he would call on his way home and ask, "What's for supper?" and I'd say, "Spaghetti," and he'd say how exhausted he was and how he wasn't even that hungry.

I noticed when he asked in the morning, "What's for supper?" and I said, "Fried cod," he would be a little happier. He would call during the day to ask, "What's for supper?" and I'd say, "Fried cod." He would say his day was okay and we'd hang up. Then he would call on his way home and ask, "What's for supper?" and I would repeat, "Fried cod. "Then he'd say he was tired but hungry.

One morning he asked, "What's for supper?" I said, "Pot roast." He jumped out of bed and skipped to the shower. He was all smiles and jokes and before he left, he asked, "What kind of pot roast?" "Pork," I told him. He skipped out to his truck and went to work. He called me halfway through the day and asked, "What's for supper?" "Pork roast," I assured him. He went on and on about how great his day was and how much he loved his job. Then he called when he left work and asked, "Are we still having pork roast for supper?" He sounded like a kid asking, "Is Santa coming tonight?"

I decided to experiment on him and started changing around some variables. In the mornings when asked, "What's for supper?" I would say, "Pot roast." He would skip to the shower as usual. Then when he called during the day to ask, "What's for supper," I would say, "Pot roast," then wait a few seconds and say, "With baked potatoes." I could hear him jumping up and down with happiness. Then he would phone on his way home and ask, "How big is the roast?" I felt like a dominatrix at this point and say, "It's massive. There may be leftovers." It would take his breath away. I thought he would pass out with happiness.

Then I would change it around and say, "Chicken." Chicken just got a yawn and an "Okay kind of day" out of him. Pasta ruined his day completely. Taking out anything for him to BBQ would make him happy, but nothing had the effect that pot-roast had on him.

Our marriage is into the second decade and I have used three full bottles of gravy browning making gravy for pot-roasts. I have friends whose marriage never made it through one full bottle of gravy browning. Maybe that was the problem.

Over the years I have learned to shake it up a bit. When he would call halfway through the day I would say, "...and I picked up a chocolate brownie cake at Sobeys for dessert."

He would run around his office giving everyone high-fives. Pull the car over on the way home and help elderly ladies cross the street. He would be giddy as a schoolgirl.

Then there would be days when I was pissed at him for something. I would take the pot-roast out of the freezer in the morning to thaw. He would phone halfway through the day and ask, "What's for supper?" and I'd say, "McDonalds!" Then he would whine and say, "But you took out a pot-roast!" I would go in for the kill and say, "I am too tired to cook it." I could hear the let-down in his voice.

I would feel empowered like the "Soup-Nazi" on Seinfeld saying, "No pot-roast for you!" The power would be all mine.

I am thinking of applying for a government grant to do an actual study on "The effects of pot-roast on men." I think it is a stupid enough idea to qualify for thousands in grant money. Then I could round up a room full of husbands and feed them pasta one night, chicken the next, then pot-roast. I would get them to fill out "Happiness charts" and measure their endorphins. I had become famous and write a book called "Saving Your Marriage with

Pot-Roast!" I would be on Dr. Phil and probably get my own reality TV show.

My mother always said, "The way to a man's heart is through his stomach." Although my sister Rose says, "The way to a man's heart is through his stomach, then you have to pull up on the knife, go through the rib-cage and then you'll get to his heart."

It is the simple things that make marriages work. He brings up my coffee every morning. I cook him a pot-roast. It's all good. It comes down to trying to figure out what makes each other happy.

For me, it is shoes. For him it is pot-roast. It works for us.

SEPTEMBER BLUES

I love September. I have always loved the beginning of the school year. New books, new clothes, new teachers and catching up with old friends. Remember sharing a pack of smokes in the high school parking lot? (I hope my kids do not read this.)

I love fall. It is my favourite time of the year. I am in my glee when the leaves start to turn orange, red, brown and yellow. There is nothing better than a walk on a cool, brisk fall day through the park. Running through my husband's fresh stack of fall leaves like a woman off her Prozac.

Except for this year.

This year September and fall sucks. I cannot seem to get my fall groove into action, and I know why. This is my son's last year of high school and my daughter's first year of junior high. It feels like the Mom Club has issued me my "Notice of Lay-off" pink slip. My days of complete control over my children are slowly slipping away and I was just getting good at it!

I got a taste of this a few years ago when my stepson finished high school and joined the Navy. It was a great relief when he picked a career, but it was hard to see him go.

I really miss him at supper time when I see his empty chair at the table. I miss his crazy sense of humour. My favourite was when hubby gained a little weight around the middle and son pointed it out to him. Hubby protested that he had not gained weight. Son said, "Oh ya. If you were standing on a beach and there were a pack of whales in the water, they would all stand up and start singing 'We are Family.'" It made me snort milk out of my nose.

God knows when I first became a mother, I did not know what I was doing. It took years to get a good system in place. I got to practice on my stepson. All I had to do was play with him all weekend and send him back to his mom on Sunday. It was not hard at all. No fighting about homework, or temper tantrums. Just feed him McDonalds and pack up his bag. He made it look so easy I decided, "Sure let's have one." Then I realized, there is no one coming on Sunday to pick this one up.

Now, sixteen years later I have a good feel for the job. If either kid filled out a "Customer Feed-Back" card I am quite sure I would be kept on and may even get a little raise on the next paycheque.

Other mothers warn you not to wish your time away when you have a baby, but the first few years have such a steep learning curve. It seems like just yesterday I learned how to use a Diaper Genie. I still gag thinking about that long line of poopy sausages and the smell that burned my eyes. It is hard not to think, "I can't wait for you to grow up!"

It seems like last night I wrote the date of my son's first smile in his baby book; the next day he was climbing down the side of the crib. Then he learned to tie his shoes and now he is going to finish high school! What the hell?

I could have sworn just yesterday I bought my daughter the most beautiful pink frilly dress for her first birthday. Then her first tooth came in. Then she lost it. Then she hated dresses. Then she liked them again. Then she hated them again. Then she dyed her hair black, became a tweenager and started junior high. I should send out an Amber Alert! The dingoes stole my babies!

I am in a complete panic. Hubby is already taking measurements to see if a hot tub will fit into my son's room.

Every chance I get I tell him, "Don't feel pressured to move out," or, "You should live home while you're going to university, it would be cheaper." Hubby is praying our son chooses to join the military because he wants to use the RESPs for a European cruise. Every chance I get I have my arms wrapped around him saying, "My baby is growing too fast! Stop it."

I cannot let go. I am going to have a complete and utter break-down if he chooses to go to university on the mainland. Then God-bless my daughter because all my craziness will be focused on her!

I understand the term "retirement." You work for thirty years. You retire and take a pension. That's life. But I did not know you could retire from being a mom.

My life revolves around being a mother! I have gone to great lengths to make sure my kids had an amazing childhood. You should drive by my house on Christmas or Halloween. People stop and take pictures of their kids on my lawn (my own kids are too embarrassed to do that anymore). My weeknights consist of driving to and from music lessons, cadets, dance, etc. I should be issued a chauffer's hat.

I have worked hard to instill a sense of family in our kids. One strict rule I have kept since the beginning is everyone eats supper at the supper table and there is no

TV, cell phones or any type of electronics allowed at my table. Violating that rule could have dire consequences. I cook a big Sunday supper every week, complete with special Sunday dishes. I have always raised my kids as "a team" as well as individuals. I make them pick up for one another and to respect each other. When my son says, "She's being a pain!" I am quick to respond with, "That's my daughter you're talking about. You better watch your mouth!" As a result, they bicker like brothers and sisters, but they also love and respect each other. We are a team! Teams do not grow up and go away!

When I think of me and hubby sitting by ourselves at the supper table with a small Sunday chicken, the waterworks start flowing! What do we talk about if the kids are gone? It is all we know. I cannot bear the thought of the kids moving out. How do I become a long-distance-mom? Can I phone my son at military school and ask him if he remembered to brush his teeth before going to bed? Will he remember to separate his whites and darks on laundry day? Will he know that there is a laundry day? Will he eat a vegetable every night if I am not there to supervise? Will his commanding officer cut up his potato for him and put butter on it before it gets too cold? He cannot live without me!

I can only imagine after a year of living on the mainland by himself he will come home thirty pounds lighter, suffering from scurvy, with underwear that have been reduced to just a thick line of elastic around his waist, his teeth falling out from decay, and his whites all grey or pink. He will beg us to let him come home and ask me to take over again, and of course I will. I am his mother, damn it. I will live my son's life for him. It is the least I could do. I will fatten him up with tablespoons of butter on his potatoes and carrots, wash his dirty clothes and put them away, make sure he brushes and flosses, and then I will find him the perfect girl to marry. That is what good mothers do!

At least that is how it plays out in my mind.

There is still hope for me. My daughter wants to be a pop star. She may be home for a while. I may even let her stay a little longer after high school if she grows out of this moody tween stage. She may even let me buy her a nice pink frilly prom dress.

It is scary becoming a new mom, but it is even scarier when you realize your days are numbered. I have always believed that the greatest gift you can give a kid is their independence.

We raise them to be good people who love themselves and the world around them. We basically work ourselves out of the greatest job on earth.

Luckily, I will always have my fourth child... hubby. He will never grow up and leave me. He does not know where his socks are without me. It only took twenty years but at least I have him toilet trained now.

When it comes to raising children, my mother used to say, "The weeks, months, and years fly by, but damn it, the days are long!"

THERE'S NO PAUSE IN MENOPAUSE!

I have been driving around the indoor parking lot at the shopping mall for about twenty minutes.

A couple comes out through the door and walks toward their car. I am parked in the middle of the lot, waiting to see where their car is. They walk past me and up to the next parking aisle. I quickly put the car in drive and whip around the corner to get to their spot. I am patiently waiting another five minutes for them to leave. Just as they pull out a little red car pulls in my parking space! I am sitting there thinking, "You saw me waiting!" A young blond woman gets out of the car and I say, "Excuse me, you saw me waiting for that spot." She smiles and gives me the middle finger then walks away.

A dark force takes over my body and I am sure this is what an out-of-body experience feels like. My face is blood red and there's steam coming out of my ears like a cartoon character. That scene from "Fried Green Tomatoes" comes to my mind. The one where Kathy Bates is in the Winn-Dixie parking lot and the two girls in the red Volkswagen take her spot. They say, "Face it, lady, we are younger and faster." Then she slams into the back of their car over and over again and says, "I am older and have more insurance."

I put the car in drive, take a deep breath.... and think about doing it. Then I realize my daughter is in the car with me and that would not be setting a good example for her. I drive away. But in my head, I ram the back of that car a dozen times screaming, "I am older, bitch, and I have more insurance!"

It is menopause, and there's no pause in menopause!

Irritability, mood swings, sudden burst of crying. They are all part of this new phase in my life.

The number one symptom... Hot flashes, cold flashes, and night sweats. God damn that Eve for eating the apple. I thought He was a merciful God. It has been centuries, how long can you hold a grudge? We bleed and cramp for half our lives and then we change over to menopause!

What the hell do men get? Bald? Really? Bald is a punishment? How is that fair? Men go through menopause, buy sports cars and date younger women. Then pretend no one notices the thirty-year age difference. Women get menopause and get an early taste of hell!

I am standing in the checkout line at Walmart. There are twenty checkouts and four are open. There is a lineup at every one of them. I finally get up to the cashier. I am next in line.

It is uncommonly hot outside for St. John's and ridiculously hot in the store. A hot flash hits. The sweat is dripping from my forehead. My hair is soaking wet and turning into a mass of curls. I could drown a small child between my breasts. The lady in front of me puts her items on the conveyor belt. She picked the one golf shirt that does not have a tag. I give her the evil eye, but it seems like the most important thing in her life is buying this golf shirt. The cashier pages someone from the men's department. Then waits.

In my head I am wrestling this woman to the ground screaming, "I got your tag right here!" She pages the salesperson again and we wait. Still no one. I am ready to start stripping in the store. My T-shirt is drenched. I am loudly tapping my fingers on the shopping cart and humming a death march while the cashier is looking nervous. She pages the salesperson again and we wait. I take the phone from her hand, hit the button, and say, "Will the incompetent fuck in the men's department who is ignoring the pages grab the $7 golf shirt and bring it over to this God damn bitch."

Luckily, I only did that in my head, not in real life. But I wanted to. It is all part of the mood swings and irritability.

Two other symptoms, fatigue and trouble sleeping.

I am so exhausted I can barely get up the stairs to the bedroom. I fall in the bed. It is 11:30 PM. Then it is midnight. Then it is 12:30. Then it's 1:00 AM. Then a hot flash hits.

Hubby has his sleep apnea machine on, and he is happily snoring away. I want to smash the clock into his face. I decide to turn on the ceiling fan instead. I pull the chain. Is it one pull or two pulls to make the air cool? I cannot remember. One pull does not seem to work. I yank it again. It is faster but I think it's going the wrong way. I yank it again and it stops. I yank it again and it goes in the other direction. I don't feel any cool air. I yank it again. It goes faster. I think the first way it spun was the right way. I yank it again. It's spinning out of control, rocking in the ceiling like it is going to take flight at any moment.

I am tired, irritable, and now my hair and nighty are soaked in sweat. Hubby wakes up to find me standing on the bed, hanging from the ceiling fan. The look on his face is sheer terror. I look like Linda Blair in the Exorcist. My head does a 360 turn, and my demon voice says, "Fix the fan or you're going to die!" He gets up and yanks the chain and it magically works. He sleeps with one eye open for the rest of the night. I just levitate above the bed.

Welcome to menopause. You have to change your underwear every time you sneeze, and you cannot remember what you were ranting about five minutes ago. I do not know why the armed forces don't recruit women going through menopause for front line duty. Can you imagine an army of us with submachine guns and tanks? "Ya, I got your peace talks right here, Mr. Taliban! Bring it on."

When does it end? Research I found says it could go on for five to ten years! But I know I am not the only one. Through my research I found the following news story from Sarasota, Florida. I say, "Go sister!"

This is a true account as recorded in the Police Log of Sarasota, Florida:

An elderly Florida lady (over 55) did her shopping and, upon returning to her car, found four males in the act of leaving with her vehicle. She dropped her shopping bags and drew her handgun, proceeding to scream at the top of her voice, "I have a gun, and I know how to use it! Get out of the car!" The four men did not wait for a second invitation. They got out and ran like mad.

The lady, somewhat shaken, then proceeded to load her shopping bags into the back of the car and got into the driver's seat. She was so shaken that she could not get her key into the ignition; for the same reason, she did not understand why there was a football, a Frisbee, and two twelve-packs of beer in the front seat!

She tried and tried, and then it dawned on her why. A few minutes later, she found her own car parked four or five spaces farther down. She loaded her bags into the car and drove to the police station to report her mistake. The sergeant to whom she told the story could not stop laughing.

He pointed to the other end of the counter, where four pale teenagers were reporting a carjacking by a mad, elderly woman described as white, less than five feet tall, glasses, curly white hair, and carrying a large handgun.

No charges were filed. If you are going to have a Menopause Moment, make it memorable!

SIX AND A BABY

We went to Mexico in early March with our whole family. I was so excited to go but not just for the hot, sunny days and clear, blue oceans. I was excited because our three kids, future daughter in-law and our seven-month-old granddaughter were coming with us. One of our sons lives in Quebec, where he attends university. Our other son and his family live in Alberta, while hubby, our daughter and I live in Newfoundland and Labrador. Getting everyone in the same place is not easy.

We were blessed with three great kids. They all get along; they are all funny and they love to hang out with one another.

We went to an all-inclusive resort on the Mayan Riviera called Occidental Grand and spent seven wonderful days playing in the sand, sitting by the pool, drinking spiced rum with pineapple juice, and even visiting one of the seven wonders of the world, a Mayan temple called Chichen Itza.

Every day I would look out at our three kids and our two newest family members and say, "Thank you, God, for this wonderful family."

Every night we would all go to supper together, each one a new culinary adventure, each one felt like Christmas dinner.

We would walk in as a group to the buffet or a la carte restaurants. The maître d' would come out in his crisp white uniform and ask, "How many?" in his thick Mexican accent and we would all reply at once, "Six and a baby."

For seven days, for breakfast, lunch, and supper we would all say, "Six and a baby." By the end of the week, it became an inside joke.

During our seven-day adventure we got to know our beautiful new grand-daughter Sophie. It was love at first site. This beautiful little creature came at a time in my life when I needed her most.

In February of 2013, my mother died, leaving a hole in my heart that I thought I could never fill. In July of 2013, Sophie was born. We finally got to meet her March 1st, 2014 at the start of our Mexican vacation. She looked at me and smiled a shy sweet smile and my heart was whole again.

She took to me right away. Constantly saying, "Nana, Nana, Nana." Which the rest thought was just gibberish, but I knew she knew who I was.

Late morning, she would take her hour-long nap and she got in the habit of falling asleep in my arms. I would lay on a chaise in the shade, put her on my chest, and she would drift off, occasionally opening an eye to look up and make sure I was there. It was the best part of my vacation.

One sunny afternoon while Sophie and I napped in the shade, I woke to see hubby and our two boys playing water polo with strangers in the pool. They were laughing and shouting and splashing each other. Our daughter and future daughter-in-law were tanning in the sun a few chairs down.

I looked out at the water and saw the most handsome man staring at me, smiling. I felt a little uncomfortable at first and I could not help but smile back. His dark, wet hair was dripping water down over his tanned face and I wondered why this man was watching me sleep with my granddaughter. My eyes finally focused, and I realized it was my husband. For a second I fell in love with a man that I had already been in love with for twenty years.

Life is good. I closed my eyes and again said, "Thank you, Jesus. Thank you, God, for this wonderful family." And just when I thought life could not get much better the pool DJ announced it was "Elvis Hour" and "Hard-headed Women" blared across the resort. I knew it was God's way of saying "Right back at ya, kid. You did well."

Saying goodbye on the last day was not easy. Putting Sophie back in her mom's arms, knowing the next time I see her she would be walking and talking, took the good out of hubby and me. They flew back to Alberta and our other son flew to Quebec. Hubby, daughter, and I boarded the plane to Newfoundland. I cried all the way back.

We arrived home Sunday night and like good Newfoundlanders our first stop was for fish and chips. Our daughter decided to stay home, so when the maître d' asked how many, it broke our hearts to say, "Two."

Every day we miss our "Six and a baby." It has now become our priority to make sure we get to do that at least once a year.

P.S. Daughter in law is pregnant again! Now it is seven and a baby!

THEY CALLED IT PUPPY LOVE

I just read an internet joke that said, "I would never feed my dog No Name dog food, but I buy No Name food for my kids all the time!"

That's me.

I think my dog Minnie May is spoiled. I named her after Elvis's grandmother, and she is a cross between a black Lab and a Terrier. If you just picture that for a moment it must have been like Fifty Shades of Grey – the dog version.

She is not a designer dog. I got her on the internet for free. My daughter begged me for two years to get a dog. She promised on her life that she would walk it and clean up after it. That lasted for about a week until she realized cleaning up after it meant picking up poop and putting it in a bag. Apparently, she did not know dogs pooped. She thought they used the toilet like her brothers. Walking and picking up poop became mom's job!

I was never a dog person. I had one years ago. It was a Dalmatian that a lawyer gave me for free. He was too busy with his law practice to take care of it. I took it not knowing what I was getting into. I should have known better than to take something free from a lawyer.

I had always been a cat person and cats do not need

anything except someone to open the food tin and clean out their litter box. Other than that, they could care less if you ever come home. Dogs are like babies. They need to be walked, cuddled, fed, and checked on every few hours.

What the lawyer did not tell me was that the Dalmatian was a thief. Insert your own lawyer joke here. Every time I let him out in the back yard he would take off and steal things from the neighbours. Every morning I would find kid's bicycle helmets, tools, teddy bears, and other items in my yard. He even stole the steak off a neighbour's grill one night! My neighbour across the street was painting her window trim and as soon as she laid the paint brush down, he stole it!

One day he came home with what looked like another teddy bear in his mouth. When he dropped it in the garden it started to run around. He stole a small dog from another yard!

The last straw came during Halloween. I let him out in the yard to pee that morning and let him in shortly afterwards.

When I left for work, I was shocked to see my lawn covered in orange Halloween garbage bags filled with leaves. He went around to all the neighbour's houses and stole their decorative Halloween bags. I had to run from house to house, putting a bag on every lawn. After that I gave him to a farmer. I never told him the dog was a thief.

I was very hesitant about taking another free dog.

For some strange reason Minnie May bonded with me. Everywhere I went, she went. If I am in the bathroom, she is outside the door. If I am washing dishes, she is asleep by my feet. Last year I had to go to Vancouver for six weeks for work. She would not eat while I was gone. I had to phone home and get my daughter to put me on the speaker phone so I could tell Minnie to eat.

After a while she grew on me. I admit I like the dog more than I like most people. Because of her I now have to go walking every day, which is good. She has become my personal trainer.

Last summer, I walked her on a walking trail around a local lake. It had rained earlier in the day and the pathway was still a little muddy. I keep a towel and a water bowl in the trunk of my car for Minnie.

I was standing at the rear of my car with the trunk open, pouring water into the dog bowl, and she jumped up into the trunk.

I dried off her feet and let her drink the water. I was just about to take the towel and put it on the front seat of my car for the dog to sit on when this man sneaks up on me and screams, "Take that dog out of the trunk!"

I was startled first, and then I started to laugh because I thought he was joking. People were looking at us. Then he yelled at me, "If you close that trunk, I'll call the cops! People like you shouldn't have dogs." Then he walked away.

I realized he was not joking. He really thought I was going to put Minnie in the trunk and drive home.

I could not get the words out of my mouth fast enough. By the time I got my thoughts together, the man was stomping all the way up the road.

People in the parking lot were whispering and looking my way. So, I loudly said, "Come on, Minnie. If you are finished with your water get in the front seat. Where you always sit. Up front with me. In the heated seats. Cause I would never lock you in the trunk." She happily jumped out and into the front seat. I tore out of the parking lot like I stole the car.

Lesson learned. Dogs are not as stupid as you think.

Up to that day she always sat in the back seat. Now she sits in the front.

When I was recovering from back surgery and on bed rest for ten weeks, Minnie May would wait for my husband to leave each morning then she would run up to our room and jump up on the bed, curling up on his side and putting her little black face on my chest. She would sit there all day, only leaving my side to bark out the window at the mailman. She hates him.

Minnie May is two and a half now and she has grown on me. I just told my daughter we can't afford to go shopping for back-to-school clothes until payday. An hour later I spent $40 on a new red dog collar covered in bling.

She knows what I am saying to her, too. I talk to her all day long. Minnie cocks her head to one side and blinks her big brown eyes and I know she is saying, "You're right, Mom!" You can see it in her eyes.

I still have a cat, Sylvester. They have worked out their living arrangements. The dog does not piss him off and Sylvester lets her live another day. Every now and then Minnie gets a little brave and tries to play with Sylvester. The cat just gives her the "Oh really!" look and she runs over to me with the "I think he likes me, Mom!" look. I have not got the heart to tell her the truth.

Now I am a dog person, too. Every day I walk Minnie around the block and see all the other dog people. Just like motorcycle drivers we wave at each other, "Hello dog person." Then we all take the most biodegradable thing in the world and put it inside the most non-biodegradable thing in the world and throw it in a land fill.

I would be lost without Minnie May now. She has become this woman's best friend and I really do like her more than most people. When I think about it, she is the only one in the world who can get me to pick up her poop!

I WON'T MARCH UNDER THE BANNER SLUT - THERE ARE BETTER WAYS TO STOP SEXUAL VIOLENCE

Oh, I can hear some of you now, "You don't support women!"

Yes, I do. I just refuse to call a woman, myself, my daughter, my mother, or my sister a slut.

Slutwalks have become the new buzz protest for women. According to their literature, participants protest against explaining or excusing rape by referring to any aspect of a woman's appearance and call for an end to rape culture.

Now, the idea behind the SlutWalk is something I will support and even protest for. Just tell me, how this is different from the "Take Back the Night" march?

I will be the first to tell you that what a woman wears at home, in a night club, walking on the street or playing hockey does not contribute to her being sexually assaulted.

If that was the case, why are Muslim women, who are completely covered from head to toe, raped? They do not show anything but their eyes and hands. So, we know that covering a woman completely still makes a man want to rape her.

The truth is, men who commit sexual assaults or rape will do it based on opportunity and gaining trust, among other things. Not on mini skirts or tube tops. They take the time to groom their victims and the family of their victims to gain their trust before taking advantage of it. Or they wait for the opportunity when their victim is weak or vulnerable, like when she is intoxicated at a party.

My problem is the word "slut." Slut is the description of herself a woman hears repeatedly when she is being held down and raped or gang raped. Slut is the reason she is given when someone she loves is punching her in the face. Slut is the nickname a young girl is given by her friends for being pretty or sure of herself. It is the name used to cut her down or put her in her place.

Slut is the last thing a woman hears when she receives the fatal blow that ends her life. Organizers of the SlutWalk says they want to "Re-appropriate the word slut" and "Take it back." But take it back to where? Re-appropriate it to what? Do they expect Oxford Dictionary to add it to their new word list?

Slut: Adjective to describe a woman in charge of her own sexuality.

The word "Rape" is never going to mean "A day at the beach."

It is never going to happen. At no point in our future will anyone walk into a class of high school girls during a career fair and say, "My, what a wonderful class of sluts. I remember when we didn't own our sexuality."

I am fifty-one years old. I have worked through the "What great legs you have, you should wear shorter skirts" 80s, the "There goes her career now that she has kids" 90s and the "There's another harassment course you have to complete this year" 2000s. I didn't kick open that glass ceiling and suffer from the cuts so my daughter can march through the streets calling herself a slut!

We are never going to change rape culture by dressing provocatively and marching with the word slut written across our breasts. We change rape culture through education and punishment. We change rape culture by talking about sexuality to our sons, brothers, fathers, uncles, and other men in our lives. Then we educate our daughters, sisters, mothers, and women in our lives about their sexuality and why we should never use the word "Slut" to describe any woman.

When the United States changed the laws to give Black people equality, those who committed hate crimes against them did not throw their hands up in the air and say, "Well we're equal now. Better leave them alone." Their hate continued; some even became more violent because they did not want the government telling them what to do.

After those laws were put in place, those people who were filled with hate had children. Their children were subjected to their parent's hate and ignorance but could see things changing. Then those children had children, and they could see the world changing. And so on. And so on. Now they have a Black President. It took generations to change the mindset.

Did it create a perfect equal world for Black people? No. There will always be people who discriminate against someone. But it made it less acceptable.

Black people did not start the "N-word march" to protest their treatment. They created the "Million Man March." They invited prominent speakers to address the audience and to convey to the world a vastly different picture of the Black male and to unite against economic and social ills plaguing the African American community.

I know what you are saying, "But Black rap artists use it in their lyrics to take back the word."

But did it work? The N-word will never be acceptable to use in any setting because we are educated now. We know what it means. Rap artists can "own it" all they want, but for millions it will always be the last name a Black man was called before he was lynched.

The same as "Slut" will always be the last name a woman is called before she is murdered. That is my opinion.

I WANT TO BE A TRAFFIC COP AT COSTCO (INSIDE THE STORE, NOT THE PARKING LOT)

My dream job is to be a traffic cop at Costco (inside the store, not the parking lot). After five minutes on the job, I would be so drunk with power.

I want one of those traffic cop whistles and a baton, too.

I would stand right at the top of the main aisle, next to the big screen TVs, blowing that whistle till I was red in the face. Only taking it out to scream, "Keep to the right. Come on, lady, keep your cart in your own lane!"

I want a ticket book, also. I would ticket people for walking too slow, letting their kids run wild, taking too many free food samples.

I would be the Costco cop from hell.

Seriously. I want Costco to hire me as their traffic supervisor. The first thing I would do is paint traffic lines on each aisle, with big white arrows pointing in opposite directions. This way people would know which side of the aisle they have to be on. There would be dotted lines, so you could pass the slow shoppers.

Then I would have parking spots painted in front of certain aisles. That way, if someone feels the need to stop and stare at the package of five hundred toilet paper rolls and try to do the math on how much they would save per roll, then they would have to pull over and get off the road to do it.

I would turn the fruit/vegetable and the milk/cheese rooms into roundabouts, just like the ones the city is putting all over St. John's. They will operate on the same principle. Each shopper will have to look to his left and yield to shoppers already in the roundabout. Once a gap in traffic appears, shoppers can merge into the roundabout and proceed to their exit. I would also have parking spots available inside each room for those people who have to stare at the lettuce and wonder if they could use fifteen heads before they rot.

The strawberry section would be a 'no stopping any time' zone. Shoppers will be forced to take the strawberries on top. There is no need to dig down to the bottom of the pile, they all came off the same truck at the same time. You will find a moldy strawberry in each one. Give it to the kid you least like.

Food sample tables would be a ten second stopping zone. That is enough time to take one cracker and a squirt of cheese then move on. You do not have to eat the entire box of crackers to see if you want to buy them. You are not some cracker connoisseur trying to figure out if the olive oil used is virgin or refined. You are from the Bay for Christ's sake. Get over yourself. It is not lunch. Move along. Nothing to see here. Repeat offenders will be prosecuted to the fullest extent of the law.

This part is ingenious: I would equip each shopping cart with indicators and bicycle bells. So, when a shopper decides they are exiting the main aisle to turn down the food processor aisle, she puts on her right indicator so the person on back of her does not shove a shopping cart up her ass.

I love the idea of bicycle bells. How many times have you been standing in the fruit/vegetable room dying of hypothermia because you are stuck behind Marge and Janet who are catching up on their grandkids? You politely say, "Excuse me?" "Excuse me?" "Can I get by you?" "Fuck Janet, call her when you get home. I'm freezing to death here!"

The bicycle bell will save you from having a complete menopausal meltdown and from getting your Costco card revoked. You just pull that little lever until the gabby gals move. Costco would sound like Christmas on steroids every day!

Do not even get me started on the parking lot. I would like Costco to block the nearest parking spaces to their building every Saturday afternoon and allow a youth group like the cadets, scouts, or a sports team to sell the parking spots off to raise money for their organization. Shoppers can buy a spot for $20 for an hour. As each shopper leaves, the spot can be resold. Cheap bastards can park over by Kent's.

I know what you are thinking: "Why doesn't she run the world?" I am wondering that myself.

I am thinking when the Costco executives read my blog they will be on the phone to their head-hunters and I'll have my contract signed by Saturday.

Oh sure, laugh now, but next Saturday when you are racing down the wrong side of the aisle to get to the huge apple pies, don't be surprised when you hear the shrill of my whistle and I pull you over near the pork chops asking, "Excuse me, ma'am, can I see your Costco card?"

WHO THE HELL GAVE ME A BABY?

I wanted children when I was a child; by the time I hit my twenties I knew it was a bad idea. I had a plant once that I called Robert, because that was the best name I could come up with. It was a cactus and it died from lack of watering.

I used to buy huge tins of cat food and dump it all in a bowl so the cat could eat all week, because I honestly thought that is how you feed cats. Then I got pregnant. My greatest fear was not gaining weight or losing weight, it was feeding the poor child. I invested in packs and packs of Post-it notes so I could leave reminders to myself each night to feed the baby the next day.

There was nothing natural about it for me. I really was a fish out of water. At the same time five other women I worked with became pregnant. Week by week they gave updates on how they loved being pregnant, how they glowed, how healthy they were eating. I hated being pregnant. I felt like an alien was growing inside me. I never glowed, my hair fell out by the handfuls in the shower, my face broke out like I was going through adolescence all over again and my feet turned into flippers. My longings were for cold spaghetti out of a tin and salsa. I never craved for apples or lettuce. Why would the good Lord pick me to give life?

The first year was hard. I had postpartum depression and my son was colic. I do not know who cried more. At the time Martha Stewart had her weekly "Living" show on TV and monthly magazines. I watched her religiously, trying to be the perfect wife and mother. I stopped watching her the night she cooked salmon over lemon tree branches that she had cut down from her garden that afternoon. I knew the bar was set too high. I would just have to do my best.

I tried to breastfeed, but the well was dry. I just could not produce enough to keep him fed. The public health nurse kept telling me, "Your milk will come in. Just keep trying. Good mothers breastfeed!" Not me. My milk stopped and the baby stopped growing, so my doctor said go to the supermarket and buy a case of Similac. Which I did. I also stopped going to the public health nurse.

My son was born in January and I was determined to get my life back. When Valentine's Day rolled around in February, I demanded that my husband and I go out as we always did. I dressed up in a silk dress and we went to our favourite Mexican restaurant. Shortly after they delivered the appetizers my husband said, "Did you spill something on yourself?" I looked down; my shirt was soaking. I ran to the bathroom. I thought I had sprung a leak. I unbuttoned the top of my dress and pulled my boobs out of my bra. My milk had come in! I looked like the Old Faithful geyser. Two steady streams of milk were hitting the cubical door and splashing on the floor. I did not know how to turn it off. I folded wads and wads of toilet paper and did something I have not had to do in years. I stuffed my bra! I folded my arms over my chest and ran through the restaurant. Our food was just arriving. "We're taking this home with us. Please pack it up!" I told the waiter, to his confusion. "I'll be in the car," I told my husband. That night, I sat in my rocking chair eating a burrito while I fed my son gallons of fresh milk. We both had gas the next day.

I remember one time the TV remote went missing for days. I tore the house up looking for it. When you have postpartum depression, you are one step away from losing it every second of every day. I blamed my husband for hiding it. (Why I thought he would do that I do not know). I cursed and swore for days, threatening to throw the TV out the window if someone did not cough up the remote. Then one afternoon, while paying for my groceries, I reached in the diaper bag for my wallet, only to find the remote. I do not know how it got there. I laid it back on the coffee table. No one said anything. They were all too afraid.

My husband worked twelve hour shifts back then and I spent a lot of nights alone. One night when my son was about eighteen months old, I gave him a bath. I laid him on the floor in my bedroom and put his diaper on him. Before I had a chance to get him in his sleepers my mother called. I was only on the phone with her for about five minutes when it struck me that he was too quiet. I hung up the phone and peeked at the bottom of the bed. He had gotten into my purse.

At that time, my husband was still a police officer, and no one could accuse me of marrying him for his money. I was on maternity leave, making only 60% of my small salary from working in radio. A new baby put a lot of pressure on the budget, so I had to watch every cent we spent. I had our monthly bills in my purse, with the cash tucked into each envelope. I planned to pay them the next day.

This was before you could pay bills by phone or over the internet.

Back then you had to drive to the utility companies.

My son had taken the money out of each envelope and was taking great pleasure in tearing each bill into pieces. Not just ripping them in half. He was making dime-size pieces of each bill. I screamed and gave him such a fright he burst into tears. I grabbed him off the floor and put him in his room, then went back to mine and, with tears hitting the carpet, tried to tape the money back together. It must have taken me a good twenty minutes to find all the pieces.

I almost had all the money put back together when my son waddled into the room saying, "I pretty, Mommy. Look at me." I looked at him in shock. He had found a blue pen and started drawing on his little fat belly, then continued down his legs and arms, onto his face and up into his scalp. I thought I was going to have a breakdown. I had to put him back in the tub and scrub till he almost bled. I am quite sure I cried more than him that night.

I always went to my mother for advice in the beginning. I figured after raising ten kids she had learned a trick or two. I dropped the baby off to her one afternoon so I could get the groceries in peace. She asked about his colic and I told her he was constipated and in pain at times, but the doctor told me he would get over it when he started to eat more. He was also teething at this point. So, all around, he was going to be a joy to baby-sit. I left the baby and diaper bag with enough provisions for a month (just in case I did not come back) and went on my way.

When I got back an hour later my mother told me she had trouble with the Pampers I had left her. She never used them before and could not figure it out. She did what she knew best. She took a small towel, folded it like an old-time cloth diaper and put it on him with two big safety pins. It was kind of funny when I looked at him sleeping in his car seat. Then it struck me. He is sleeping!

"How long has he been sleeping?" I asked. "Oh, about a half an hour." Bewildered, I asked how she got him to sleep. "Just an old trick from back home. You said he was teething, so I rubbed his gums with brandy, and he fell off shortly after that."

"You gave my baby brandy?" "Don't be so foolish, that's what you're supposed to do with teething babies."

Disgusted, I left her house to drive home with my baby passed out in his car seat. I was no more than two minutes away from her house when I got the smell. It was pure sewer! Then I heard this loud gurgling noise, and the smell filled the car. "Did I walk in dog crap," I thought. Then I heard a fart a grown man would be proud of and I looked in the rear-view mirror. He was still asleep, but he was smiling. By the time I got home my eyes were burning.

I opened the side door of the van and released him from the safety harness. He had diarrhea. The car seat was full of it. It was down his legs and the cloth diaper did nothing to hold it in. It dripped over the car seat and onto the floor. I had to hold him by the armpits at arm's length to carry him. I forgot to take the house key out of my pocket, so I had to hold him with one arm while trying to unlock and open the house door. It was then another loud fart hit, and a litre of diarrhea flowed down his leg, onto my hip and down my leg.

By the time I got to the bathroom we were both covered from head to toe with liquid shit! I had to take everything he and I were wearing off and throw it in the garbage. Then we both got in the shower.

When we got out, I laid him on a towel on the floor while I tried to dry myself. I heard another big fart, so I grabbed him and held him over the toilet. I spent the next half hour sitting naked on the bathroom floor, holding my naked son over the toilet, thinking each time, "There can't possibly be more!"

I finally got him in a real diaper and both of us dressed. I phoned my mother and told her off for giving him brandy.

"That wasn't the brandy," she informed me, "that was the prunes. I fed him a great big jar of baby food prunes to cure his constipation." For the next two days, I could not leave the house and he lost about five pounds.

The one thing I learned through it all is, do not sweat the small stuff. I was on my way to work one morning when I noticed chocolate around a fingernail. While manoeuvring through early morning traffic, I licked it off. Then thought, "I hope it was chocolate." I ran through my agenda that morning: fed the baby, changed the baby, got dressed and left the house. Don't remember eating chocolate.

Oh well.

THE BOY'S CAT

It is the insatiable crying that drives me mad.

Every night she walks from room to room searching and crying. It is like she knows when I am just about to doze off.

She sits by the side of my bed. She knows I let one hand hang over the side, and she arches her back until my fingers are running through her fur. She turns around and puts her head under my hand, forcing me to scratch her behind the ears.

She came to us by accident. My mother's cat had kittens. My son was almost three at the time. He fell in love with the long-haired ginger curled up in the cardboard box. Nan said he could have her.

She slept on his bed. As he grew, she grew. She followed him around the house and waited for him to come home from school each day. She went to bed when he did, snuggling into his back or stretched out on top of him. Leaving a trail of fur all over his bedspread.

He played X-box with her sitting in his lap or lounging next to him. He rubbed her fur without knowing it and scratched her head instinctively.

I have never had to do anything for her. She was not my cat. I do not know why she seeks me out at midnight every night. She stares directly into my eyes, meowing like she is asking me a question. "What do you want?" I ask her, exasperated by her relentless crying. She asks again but I don't understand. She follows me around the house all day long, crying and crying. It never stops. She is not hungry, or sick. I don't know how to pacify her.

I turn the key to the front door. The sun is shining in through the foyer window onto the slate floor. I open the door and she is enjoying the sun rays, stretched out like she is laying on a beach. When I come in, she jumps up and swirls around my feet. I scratch her head hello and go into the kitchen. I get her food and lay it on the floor, but she does not go near it.

I can hear the school bus stopping at the top of the street. She scratches frantically at the door to get out and I open it to let her go. I watch her cross the street and run like a cheetah to the corner. She greets the bus. The driver opens the door, and the children pile out. She sits, watching each child walk by. Some stop and scratch her head and her tail sways in appreciation. The last of the children get off and the door closes. The bus pulls away. She is still sitting there. Waiting.

The last boy off the bus rubs her head then walks down the street towards his house. She follows him. He turns around and smiles. He waits for her to get near, then reaches down and scoops her up in his arms. She nuzzles into his neck. The boy strokes her back and her long tail sways around his waist in glee.

He gently lays her down on the sidewalk as he gets closer to his house. She sits and watches him go inside. She gets up and meanders across the street to our house and paces in front of the door as if to say, "I am home now." I let her in and as I close the door, she locks eyes with me, meowing and crying all at once. Asking me the same question she asks every night when I am trying to sleep. I don't know how to get it through to her. She never gives up asking. She never stops crying.

Frustrated with my response, she bows her tail and runs to the basement. I follow her down there to see what she is doing. I don't go down there anymore. She leaps up on the couch and curls into the abandoned white hoodie bunched up in the corner. It is covered in fur. She has slept there before. I should throw it out, but I cannot. She smells him on it. I sit next to her and scratch her head. She begins to cry again. Asking the same question. I tell her repeatedly, but she does not get it.

He is gone, I tell her. She cries again and it sounds like "Why? Why?" She crawls onto my lap, arching her back like a Halloween cat and then reaching her cold nose up till it touches mine. Her eyes are green, and she locks them on mine. "Where is he?" she asks. I tell her every day, "The boy is gone. You have to learn to let go."

She walks off my lap and back to the hoodie. Laying down with her back towards me. I know she is saying, "I don't believe you."

Suddenly she jumps to her feet and runs up the stairs. I can hear her scratching at the front door. I chase after her. I can hear the second school bus at the top of the street. I open the door and she runs up to the bus stop. The doors open and she sits patiently. Watching the kids get off. The doors close and the bus pulls away. She gets up and begins the slow walk back to her house. Her tail is down, and I can see her mouth moving. She is crying again.

I let her back in. I hate the sound of the school bus. I miss the boy too. I long to see him jump off the bus with his heavy book bag over his shoulder. Running towards home and her running after him.

She searches the house again. Looking for him. I follow her to the basement; now an empty, hollow room filled with electronic games, a TV and couch. The walls are a shrine to his accomplishments. Certificates and trophies are everywhere.

She is crying. "Where is he?" She leaps back to the couch and curls up in the boy's hoodie. I lay on the couch and she climbs on top of me. I cry with her.

"Where is he? Where is my baby boy?" The tears sting my eyes and roll down my cheeks. She lifts her head and meows back to me, "Why? Why?"

She jumps off and runs upstairs again. I go behind her.

She is scratching at the door again. She wants to go out. I open the door. There is a group of boys heading to the park. She chases after them. They do not notice her trailing behind.

I can hear her cry. I know what she is saying. "Do you know where my boy is?" They do not pay any attention to her.

She will keep me up again tonight. Continuously crying. Like me. Asking, "Where is my boy?"

A GAME OF THONGS

I just bought my first pair of black leggings or jeggings. I am not sure what they are called anymore. I want to have an option instead of wearing the same jeans everyday (even though I have fifty pairs in my closet).

All the fashion magazines have models wearing comfy sweaters, huge scarfs tied around their necks that look like blankets, and black leggings, usually in leather but that is only because they don't live in a Northern climate like me. Wearing leather leggings in my Canadian climate during the fall literally means you will freeze the ass off yourself.

Even with all that wool surrounding their bodies, they still look like they have not eaten in months. I cannot pull that off.

A good friend of mine told me spandex is a privilege not a right, and unless I have been doing a hundred squats a day, I should stick to breathable cotton.

So breathable cotton leggings it is.

Leggings are basically black pantyhose with no feet. It is not like sliding on jeans. I have to sit down on a chair just to pull them over my feet. Then I inch them up my legs, over my hips and around my waist. It is a good twenty-minute workout.

I finally got them on only to discover I have two big problems:

1. Camel toe. (To save you the trouble of Googling it, Wikipedia says "Camel toe is a slang term that refers to the outline of a woman's labia majora, as seen through tightly fitting clothes. Due to a combination of anatomical factors and the tightness of the fabric covering it, the crotch and mons pubis may take on a resemblance to the forefoot of a camel. Camel toe commonly occurs as a result of wearing tight fitting clothes, such as shorts, hotpants or swimwear." Not sure when they updated that last, but I have not worn "hotpants" in a long time. Plus, my labia majora looks more like elephant foot than camel toe in leggings.

2. I literally have my panties in a bunch. You can see the outline of my underwear through the leggings! The last thing I need is some pervert fantasizing about my granny panties when I am stylin' in my fashionable leggings with a blanket wrapped around my neck.

So, I Googled "How do you hide your underwear when wearing leggings?" Google came back with a list of websites to help women hide VPLs (Visible Panty Lines). Yes, apparently that is another thing we have to deal with.

The bottom line is, VPLs are best hidden by wearing a thong.

That's right, ladies, a thong.

Now, I have already invested $40 in a pair of leggings, so I am going to have to check out the thongs.

Anyone who knows me knows I am big fan of comfortable underwear. Not just any comfortable underwear but they also have to hide the fact that I have had two children (both fat babies), possible cellulite (caused by said fat babies), bought a gym membership but will never use it, loves to eat, hates sit-ups, and they have to make me look like a Victoria's Secret Model.

But to wear these leggings I will participate in this "Game of Thongs."

Off to Victoria's Secret I go.

I take the leggings with me and show them to the teenage salesgirl. I educate her on camel toe and my panties being in a bunch, then ask for her expert opinion, as a Victoria's Secret Salesgirl, on recommending a thong for a fifty-one-year-old woman.

I know she is screaming in her head, "I make minimum wage! I shouldn't have to deal with this crap!" I lean in and whisper, "I've been waxed. Full Brazilian. Don't worry, I can do this." I cannot explain the look of horror on her face.

She politely takes me to the thong section of the store, then picks out some of the "best sellers" for me to try on, then whispers, "Over your panties!" I guess she did not believe the whole "I have been waxed" line.

I go into the change room and pull the thong on over my panties, then the leggings, but that was stupid because now you can see the panties and the thong, and it looks like I am wearing a diaper. I decide to just give in and buy the thong so I can try it on at home. Apparently the smaller the underwear the more expensive they are because the thong was almost $15.

At home I decide to get ready for the fall runway. I put on my new thong and the leggings. Google was right! There are no panty lines. I am happy that I can wear my leggings without the dreaded VPLs plaguing womankind.

Now, I am an all-or-nothing kind of girl. No allowing

time to break these babies in. I am walking the dog.

Word of advice. Do not walk the dog while wearing a thong!

Ten minutes into our walk I start to feel like I invented the yeast infection. Twenty minutes into the walk I felt like I had performed surgery on myself. By the time I got home it felt like I had given birth to a hippo.

It took another twenty minutes to find the thong and get it off. I may need stitches.

Who created the thong anyway? I could only imagine some French guy with weird bondage issues.

I went back to my comfortable underwear, spent another twenty minutes pulling the leggings back on, and stared at my camel toe.

Then I had what Oprah would call an "A-ha moment." I discovered the cure for VPLs.... long sweaters. That is how you get rid of camel toe.... long sweaters!

I win the game of thongs!

DO YOU REMEMBER WATERBEDS? BOW CHICK A WOW WOW

When my husband and I moved in together, he convinced me to buy a waterbed.

It seemed like a good idea at the time.

I know, insert the 'bow chick a wow wow' here.

Remember the waterbed? It had a vinyl water-filled bladder with a temperature control device that was supposed to synchronize with human body temperature.

Waterbeds were all the rage back then. It was the 90s. Everyone had shoulders pads, big hair, and waterbeds.

It was reported that Hugh Hefner had a huge waterbed at the Playboy Mansion covered in Tasmanian possum hair. Can you just picture Hugh with his hairy chest and captains hat laying naked on his possum hair waterbed.

I know what you are thinking.... Growwwllll. I am coughing up a fur ball just thinking about it.

Anyway, hubby insisted that it was the only bed he could sleep on, so when we moved in together, I gave in and agreed to the waterbed.

It was the old-fashioned waterbed that had the big wooden frame around it and a bookshelf headboard. It took up most of the bedroom. There was no changing the room around once it was filled. A hundred men could not shift it an inch.

Back then hubby worked shifts and would often come home when I was still sleeping. This bed did not have the wave control that later models had. He would try to tiptoe into the bed but the slightest movement at all sent me flying into the air and I would end up on the floor beside the bed. On the way down to the floor I would hit something, an elbow, a knee, or my face, on that wooden frame.

He said it was like sleeping on a big cruise ship. I thought it was more like victory at Sea.

Then we moved.

It took longer to move that bed than anything else in the house. It took a full day just to drain it! Then we had to take the bed frame apart and pack it all up.

Setting it up in the new house also took a day. We had to run the garden hose from the bathroom to the bedroom and hook it up to the mattress. That was after we spent a day putting that huge bedframe together.

One of us had to stay in the bathroom to make sure the hose did not come undone while the other one waited in the bedroom making sure the connection to the mattress didn't come undone.

You could hear the floorboards creaking as they tried their best to hold the extra 2,000 pounds of weight.

We finally got rid of it when I was pregnant.

At around the eighth month mark I was as big as a whale. I could not wear my own shoes anymore because my feet looked like flippers. I had to wear hubby's sneakers around the house. I could barely get in and out of a chair, let alone a waterbed.

One night while hubby was working, I went to go to bed. At this point, it was like a diving exercise. I would sit on the side of the bed and fall backwards. The waves would carry me in, so I could haul my bloated legs on board.

It took a good fifteen minutes to get my pregnant body lined up in the middle. Once I finally got settled, I had to pee. That started the whole process of trying to get out of the bed. Remember, this waterbed was one of the old ones that did not have the wave control or back support. It was just a big bladder filled with water.

I tried to roll over on my side, but I could not get my body to roll. The extra weight around my middle was keeping me anchored down. I tried rolling to the other side with the same response. I was flopping around like a fish out of water.

I was trapped in the middle of it! Like a big pregnant turtle on her back.

Flailing around in the bed like that on top of a big giant bladder only made my pregnant bladder scream, "Empty me now!"

I tried to reach the phone on the nightstand to call for help. I was able to reach the receiver and knock it off the cradle, but instead of falling into the bed, it fell on the floor. This was before cell phones. So now in addition to being held captive on a waterbed and holding my pee, I had to listen to the beep, beep, beep from the phone being off the hook. God love the 90s!

I was detained against my will on the Good Ship Lollipop for about an hour. By the time I broke free my own bladder was busting.

Hubby was working the all-night shift and by the time he got home the next morning I had the bed drained and the bladder rolled up in the front hall.

Never underestimate the strength and determination of a woman who is eight months pregnant.

That afternoon we went to Sears and picked out a chiropractic, pillow top queen mattress. I remember crawling in bed that night feeling like God himself was cradling my lower back under all that pregnant weight.

To this day he still wishes he had the waterbed because he would sleep better.

That is not going to happen.

I think that idea has sprung a leak.

THE SISTERHOOD OF W.I.N.E. WOMEN IN NEED OF EXCITEMENT.

"Maybe our girlfriends are our soul mates, and guys are just people to have fun with." -- Sex and the City.

Remember back in high school? You had so many girls who were friends. The friends I walked to school with, friends I had lunch with, friends I met after school, friends I went out with on the weekends. I always had lots of girlfriends. After high school, we stayed friends. Many a Friday and Saturday night we closed down a night club. Then walked up Long's Hill in three-inch stilettos, in the wintertime, went to a restaurant for late-night food, and staggered home at 4 AM.

Next weekend we did it all over again. We laughed. We shared secrets. We had great times... and then we grew up.

Today I could not walk up Long's Hill in sneakers or eat food at three in the morning without ending up at the Emergency Department in a hospital.

Times have changed.

I met a new best friend: My husband. Over twenty years later, we are still best friends. We raised three kids together. We built our careers together. We built our home together. We travel together. We shop together. We eat together. We sleep together. We do everything together. We are BFF's till the end. And that is the way it should be.

But between raising kids, keeping the marriage strong and focusing on my career, I lost track of my girlfriends. Not to say I still do not have them. I do, but not like it used to be. I have met some great women over the years. Most of my friends are the mothers of my children's friends. I do not see a lot of people that I went to high school with anymore and I don't have that same high school relationship with women I meet now.

Now that the kids are older – one has moved out, one is going to finish high school next year, and one is going to junior high – I find myself with lots of free time, especially on the weekends.

We no longer need babysitters, and our kids have their own plans for Friday and Saturday nights.

We usually find ourselves looking at each other, saying, "What do you want to do?" "I don't know." "What do you want to do?"

My husband has no interest in going to Pier 1 to see what is new or rummaging through Winners for the latest sales. Those are the times I really miss having a female BFF like I used to. I think a lot of women go through this. We devote ourselves to our children, our careers, our marriages. Everything but ourselves. Then the children grow up, our careers are getting close to retirement, and our husbands are more interested in golf than shopping. We find ourselves going through our Facebook friend list thinking, "I wish I had stayed in contact with her."

I love watching "Sex and the City." It is my favourite show. I think the reason so many women love this show, besides the great writing and the funny repertoire between the characters, is the relationship between the women. We would all like to have a relationship like these four women. These women never judge each other. They never backstab. They are there for each other during every crisis. Even though the characters represent four vastly different women, they never sacrifice who they really are because someone else has a problem with it.

My sister gave me a sign for my kitchen as a gift. It is a lady sitting at a bar holding a glass of wine and the writing above her head says, "The sisterhood of W.I.N.E. – Women In Need of Excitement." Below that it says, "Welcoming new members since the beginning of wine."

It got me to thinking.

I think a lot of women are looking for the sisterhood of W.I.N.E. – Women In Need of Excitement. Women who want to get back to having girlfriends that they can talk to and laugh with. We just need to learn to do for ourselves what we have been doing for others. When my daughter went to kindergarten, she was very shy and found it hard to make friends. Every day I would tell her, "To get a friend, you have to be a friend." Now I find I am saying it to myself.

I am setting up my own sisterhood of W.I.N.E., women who get together to celebrate their accomplishments and talk about their lives at a table where they will not be judged, where they won't be talked about, where they feel welcome.

Everyone is welcome. If you are interested in being in the sisterhood, let me know and I'll tell you when the next meeting is.

THEN A HERO COMES ALONG

Not all heroes wear their underwear on the outside or fly around in capes wearing spandex.

Most live their lives quietly, not knowing that anyone is watching.

My friend Sondria writes a blog called "The Rising." It is about her life with breast cancer. I love reading it because it not only inspires me, but it also gives me a kick in the ass when I need one.

Believe it or not, there are lots of days when I need a good kick in the ass to get going. I went through major back surgery a few years ago and I am still recovering, still living in pain, and this damp, cold weather does not make life any easier. There are days I just cannot take the pain anymore.

Then a hero comes along.

Sondria posts a blog. It is about her daily struggles with breast cancer. She is funny and witty. She makes me laugh out loud. I look through her pictures documenting her past year. The picture of her beautiful daughter. I cannot imagine what goes through your mind when you're fighting for your life. I know her first thoughts have to be about her daughter and the life she only started to live. I cannot even get my mind around it. She puts herself out there. She is not afraid to cry out loud. She lets a photographer take her picture showing her reconstructed breast to the world.

I sit up and think, how lucky am I? My back hurts. So, what. Get up and get moving. It is not cancer. Thank you, Sondria, for kicking my ass.

It is so easy to let yourself get down. I still have a hard time walking and doing stairs sometimes. It gets frustrating because I used to run five miles every day. I ran a ten-mile road race! Now sometimes I need help going down the stairs. Without even thinking, I start with the, "Why me? Why did this happen to me?"

Then a hero comes along.

My mother-in-law died in 2014. A few years before she died, her leg had to be amputated to save her life. It was extremely hard on her. She was a beautiful woman who loved to dance, to go shopping, to go bowling every week. Then a horrible disease took her leg and gradually weakened the remaining one. She used a walker to get around, but most of the time she used a wheelchair.

A traumatic blow like that could send someone into a deep depression; not her. She got up every morning, put on her make-up, did her hair, and would call the wheelchair shuttle service when she wanted to go out. She refused to be a burden to anyone and insisted on living alone. She was gone all the time, playing cards, visiting friends, going to supper. Her will to live was incredible. I've never heard her say, "Why me? Why did this happen to me?" She just smiles and says, "Thank God I am alive. Every day is a blessing." The wheelchair did not define who she was or what she could do. It is just a chair.

I think of her when I get frustrated and tell myself, take the ramp. Who needs stairs anyway? Be grateful you can still walk.

The one thing I have realized over the past year is that no one suffers from an illness alone. It affects everyone around you. Your children, your coworkers, your friends, your spouse.

Then a hero comes along.

I would never be able to have the quality of life I have now without my husband. He suffers from this disease as much as I do. Over the years, we have developed a love of travel and used to take the opportunity every chance we could. It is hard to travel with someone who can't walk long distances and needs a cane from time-to-time. I am sure he never imagined his life would end up like this. I have learned that you have to compromise to make a marriage strong.

I have also learned that you have to say, "Thank you." There are times when I have to cancel our plans at the last minute because I am not feeling well. There are times I cannot get out of bed and my husband becomes a single parent, having to leave work early to drive kids to events, finish homework and make supper. I realize you cannot help it when you're sick, but you can say, "Thank you," to those around you who are also affected by your illness.

Having a disease does not make you a hero. It just makes you a person with a disease. How you deal with it makes you a hero. How you treat the people around you makes you a hero.

The people in your life that allow you to continue to live with dignity, who live with your disease, too, they are the heroes. Make sure you thank them every day.

THE DRESSES OF A WOMAN'S LIFE

My daughter picked up her prom dress this week. We have been waiting five months for its delivery like expectant parents. Getting the right dress was like finding the Holy Grail. She looked at hundreds of dresses in every colour and style. Each time she went into the dressing room to try one on, I would wait outside with my fingers crossed praying, "Please God, let this be the one." I walked thousands of miles through shopping malls and bridal stores, getting carpal tunnel syndrome from my arms being in the air, searching through racks of formal dresses saying, "What about this one?"

The day she bounced out of the dressing room in a beautiful simple black dress, smiling ear to ear, and said, "This is the one," was the happiest day of my life. Getting the right prom dress is extremely important to a girl. That dress tells the world that she is transitioning from a high school girl to a young woman. The pictures of her wearing it will be something she treasures forever.

It made me think of all the other dresses that are so important in a woman's life. When my daughter was born, I wanted her to have the most beautiful christening dress. I cannot remember what it cost but I'm sure I spent a small fortune on it. The sweater, bonnet and bootees were hand knit by a friend of our families. Now the whole lot of it is wrapped in blue paper and sealed in a plastic container. Someday I will take it out and give it to her when her baby is christened someday.

The next dress I bought her was her school uniform. It was a standard, navy blue tunic, like the one that I wore when I started kindergarten. She wore a crisp white blouse, navy blue socks, black patent leather shoes, and I put her hair up in pigtails, which was the cause of a huge fight that morning. But when she came down over the stairs with her pigtails bouncing and her smart school uniform, she looked like a little doll. I could not wait to take her to my mother's house and show her off. Her school tunic told the world that she was now ready to be educated. A privilege that so many girls in this world do not get to experience.

She starts university in September, and I guess the next dress will be the university graduation dress, followed by the wedding dress.

Thinking about it made me go through my own closet of memories.

I still have my prom dress. It is in a plastic bag, tucked into the back of my closet. My mother and I designed it ourselves by going through stacks of Simplicity dress patterns we found in the upstairs of the Arcade on Water Street. We mixed and matched dresses until we had the perfect skirt and top. Then we found a seamstress who put it together. It was grey taffeta with a princess skirt. It was the first real dress I ever owned. When I put it on, on the day of my prom, along with makeup and my hair locked tight with Final Net, I looked in the mirror and realized that this dress would show the world that I had left my tomboy phase behind and really was a girl.

Next came the dress I bought to snag the man I knew was going to be my husband. I banked on that little black dress making him fall in love with me. I spent half my paycheque on that dress. I bought it at Le Château, and I knew when I looked in the dressing room mirror that an engagement ring would not be far behind. It was worth every cent because I knew from the look on his face when he saw me that it was mine – hook, line, and little black dress!

Then came the wedding dress. I designed it myself and worked with a seamstress. I read thousands of bridal magazines and tore out stacks of pages of dresses that I liked. I knew I wanted something off the shoulder and a skirt that was straight. I did not want anything puffy. I went back-and-forth with the seamstress for months. Finally, she delivered the dress of my dreams. I will never forget the look on my husband's face when I walked down the aisle. My dress was beautiful, with a train that followed behind me and a veil of white lace framing my face. My future husband was smiling from ear to ear and wiped away a tear. This dress told the world that I was now a wife.

That dress was followed by a power suit. A new addition to my life. It had a navy-blue skirt and blazer, and I matched it with a white blouse and matching navy-blue stilettos. It was meant to impress those on the hiring board and tell them I was a professional lady who would be a great addition to their organization. The power suit was a new kind of dress for me but one that became my own uniform for years and served me well. It told the world that I was ready to take it on and win.

The day finally came for a different kind of dress. My first maternity dress, which I bought at Zellers. It was a replica of one Princess Diana wore. It was red with a princess collar and a little black velvet ribbon tied around the collar. It made me look as big as a house and I cried when I put it on. But I was incredibly proud to wear it. I knew wearing this dress was an honour that so many of my friends would never have due to infertility and other medical issues. I put my big, red, flowing tent of a dress on with pride. It told the world that I would soon be the best mother in the world.

Then there was that after-the-baby-was-born dress. It took a few months before I wore that one. It was two sizes bigger than the dress I wore before pregnancy. I hated that dress. It told the world that I did not lose the baby weight and that my body was now going to be a new size. A motherly size.

Then there is the yo-yo dress. That is the dress I bought after I lost the baby weight, which told the world I was back on track.

Then there was the dress that was three sizes bigger than my wedding dress, that which told the world it was unrealistic for me to expect stay the same size I was when I got married.

Then there was the dress that was bigger than that one. It told the world I loved potato chips more than I loved my figure.

The dress after that one was two sizes smaller. It told the world I had found Weight Watchers.

The dress after that one told the world I was now going to have a yo-yo weight that went up and down for the rest of my life.

I was incredibly proud of the dress I wore to my son's high school graduation. I did not care what size it was. It was a big day to watch my firstborn graduate from high school, and I cried the day I put that dress on. It told the world how incredibly proud I was of him.

Then there is the dress I wore at my twentieth wedding anniversary. That night we went to the Keg for supper and reminisced about everything we had achieved over the years. We raised our children to be good people, kept a marriage together, built a wonderful home that we both loved, and reminisced about the beautiful journey we had taken together. That dress told world I was now comfortable and confident with who I was.

This month I will shop for two dresses: one I wear to my daughter's graduation from high school, and one I wear to my son's convocation from university. I am really looking forward to wearing those dresses. They tell the world that my children are successful and moving forward in life. They also tell the world that my husband and I have done our jobs as parents and helped our children achieve their goals.

In between all these dresses there have been so many others: Christmas party dresses, New Year's Eve gowns, summer dresses, winter dresses, spring dresses.

So many dresses that define the life of a woman. What I have learned from all these dresses is, even though a good dress can make you feel beautiful, powerful, successful, proud, and even magical, a dress cannot define who you are. It is your hard work, values, beliefs, and actions that tells the world who you really are.

The dress is just the frame for that picture.

MISGUIDED MESSAGES

I really do have a medical condition that causes memory loss. I cannot blame it all on menopause. This condition creates daily hurdles for me to jump over, so I came up with a few coping strategies to help me remember things. One of those strategies is to email myself. This is normally done on the fly using the mic on my iPhone. For example, when I am getting out of the shower and remember I need to pick up milk, or when I am just about to start a yoga class and remember I need to sew the hole in the fork of my yoga pants, I will just send myself a quick email using the phone's mic. So, when I look at my phone later, I will remember to buy milk and wear underwear to yoga.

The problem with this strategy is I do not always take the time to make sure I have selected MY email address or that autocorrect understands my Newfoundland accent.

A few days ago, I received an email from a friend who had typed, "Stay strong. I am surprised, but I'll support you no matter what you decide." I was confused at first. Then I scrolled down through her message and discovered the email I thought I sent to myself earlier that day had been sent to her by mistake. The email I sent to me was, "To do today: clean out hubby and my closet. Bag and bring to goodwill." The email SHE received said, "Today told hubby I am out of the closet. Sad to tell him I am Bill."

Well, as you can imagine, I had to make a quick phone call and go into damage control mode before word got around. I thanked her for the support but assured her the occasional facial hair was from menopause not hormones. We had a good laugh, and I made a mental note to read emails before I sent them.

Of course, I forgot that note five minutes after I hung up the phone.

A good friend of mine is a priest. Last year I accidentally sent him an email that said, "Why do I sweat more under my boobs than my armpits?" I had met with my doctor a month before about controlling some annoying menopause symptoms. She had put me on a new drug but told me to keep track of the symptoms and any questions I had for my next appointment. That morning the annoying symptom was boob sweat. My priest friend emailed me back with, "I don't know but I'll pray for you." Can you just picture this poor man on his knees, holding Rosary beads and chanting, "Please Lord Jesus give us world peace, stop the suffering of little children, and cure Helen's boob sweat."

This morning was the worst. I can no longer leave my house. I have also banned myself from email. I woke up to an email from my former boss, who is a high-ranking officer in the RCMP. All the email said was, "???? Did you mean to send this to me?" I jumped out of bed and scrolled down through the message. Last night, before I fell asleep, I sent myself an email that said, "How do you cure vaginal dryness?"

Oh, sweet hearted, jumping in the garden Jesus!!! I cannot believe I did that!!!

I had to send him back an email that said, "Sorry. That was meant for me only. (P.S. was asking for a friend)."

Moral of the story is: if you ever get an email from me that seems a little weird or embarrassing, please delete it and do not answer it. Or, if someone tells you I am a lesbian with boob sweat and a dry vagina, please tell them you have it from a good source that rumour is not true.

WHY I TIP THE SCHOOL BUS DRIVER

I am a good tipper when I get good service. I always remember to tip my manicurist so when I break a nail or need to move an appointment, she bends over backwards to accommodate me. I tip well at restaurants, too, because I have worked as a waitress and I know how hard that job is. I also do not want anyone spitting in my food the next time I go there. Tipping is a way of showing your appreciation when someone goes above and beyond their job.

The most important person I tip is the school bus driver.

It is more like a gift/tip thing I started doing shortly after my kids started school. I always give the school bus driver a gift card from the liquor store for Christmas, Easter, and at the end of the school year.

Now I know parents are thinking, "I have enough people to buy for. I am not including the bus driver!"

As a parent, I assure you that the school bus driver is the most important person on your list. We are incredibly lucky to have a great driver in our neighbourhood who controls the bus and we have never had an incident while he has been driving.

This past Friday, my husband looked out the front window and said, "Why is there a school bus in front of our house?" The kids had come home ten minutes earlier. The doorbell rang and Paul, the driver, passed over my son's coat and said, "He left that on the bus." My husband remarked, "That was nice of him to do that." "That's why I always tip the bus driver," I informed him.

When my kids started school, they went through hats and gloves like water. I could buy them by the truck load. Every day they would leave something on the bus: a book bag, a cell phone, and their head. It was never ending.

Then there is the morning race to make it to the bus on time.

How many times did I show up late for work because the kids missed the bus and I had to drive them? Now I do not mind driving my kids to school. It is that darn Kiss'n'Ride lane I hate. If you take a second longer than you have to those bitches will gang up on you. One morning, a lady (I use that adjective loosely) rolled down the window of her SUV and screamed at me, "Get the lead out of your ass! I gotta go to work." All I wanted was an extra kiss from my daughter and ended up getting bitch-slapped by a blond.

I know being a school bus driver is a hard job. It takes a special person to be able to drive all those kids from neighbourhood to neighbourhood in the morning, while keeping them in their seats, keeping the peace and trying to stay on the road. I would not make a good school bus driver because I would be kicking kids off at every corner.

When Paul took over our route about five years ago, I noticed a remarkable improvement in the service. If my kids were not at the bus stop, he would stop as he drove by our house and blow the horn. Either my husband or I would poke our head out and say, "They're sick," or

"We're coming!" If the kids left something on the bus, he would make sure they got it back the next day.

My son, who has a huge interest in politics, sits up front so he can discuss political issues with Paul on the way to school.

Paul's good service makes my life easier. Like most people who have decided to make a career out of taking care of our children while we work, bus drivers do not make a lot of money. When you are lucky enough to have one that goes above and beyond, you show your appreciation.

A small token during the holidays and at the end of the year means my son's hundred-dollar winter coat gets delivered to my door and my kids never miss the bus. Thanks, Paul. Please do not retire until my daughter finishes high school.

WHY YOU SHOULD MARRY YOUR BEST FRIEND*

*Written in 2012

I woke up this morning with socks on my feet. They were not there last night when I went to sleep. I was a little surprised when I woke up this morning to find someone had put them there.

I just had surgery a few weeks ago on my back and I cannot bend, drive, or lift anything over five pounds. I cannot reach my feet. After I got out of bed, I noticed that my hair dryer and straightening iron had been laid out on a bench next to my makeup dresser.

When I got to the kitchen the coffeepot had already been set up; all I had to do was press the on button.

Then it struck me. Before my husband left for work, he set up the coffee for me. He had laid out my straightening iron and curling iron on a bench that he had brought into the room, knowing I could not pick them up off the floor. He had slipped socks on my feet knowing I could not do it myself.

This says a lot about a man. He knew the limitations that I would be faced with on the morning of my first day alone after leaving the hospital. He had to go back to work and the kids had to go to school. He knew I would not be able to get my own socks on. He knew that I would want to put on my makeup and do my hair. He knew I loved my morning coffee, and he had that ready for me. He knew exactly what I wanted.

The one thing that saves a marriage is dignity. When you take away a person's dignity it can never be restored. When you give a person their dignity, you create a foundation that keeps marriages alive.

There is a lot of good reasons for getting married and there's a lot of bad reasons for getting married. I was lucky enough to marry my best friend and eighteen years later we remain best friends. I cannot think of one time when we've actually had a screaming, yelling fight. We just do not do that; we respect each other too much. We love each other too much.

Over the past eighteen years I have discovered that love is not about roses or chocolates on Valentine's Day. Love is about giving a person their dignity. It is about knowing someone has your back. It is when you have back surgery, and you can't go to the bathroom by yourself and you need help.

It is when your partner doesn't roll their eyes and allows you to keep your dignity during those times. It is when you wake up in excruciating pain from back surgery to find out your husband has set up the coffee for you and laid out your hair dryer and straightening iron. It is when you wake up with socks on your feet.

That is when you know marrying your best friend was a good idea.

WOMEN HOLD UP HALF THE SKY

I was watching Oprah Winfrey one afternoon; her guests were Nicholas D. Kristof and Sheryl WuDunn, authors of a book called, "Half the Sky: Turning Oppression into Opportunity for Women Worldwide." Their story was so compelling that I went out and bought the book and read it over the following two days.

As women, we have no idea how lucky we are to be born free in Canada, and this book opened my eyes to several atrocities committed against women around the world.

The title comes from a Chinese proverb that states, "Women Hold up Half the Sky." After reading this book and informing myself on global issues that women and children face every day, I have decided that when you commit violence towards one woman, you commit violence against us all. We have a duty to stand up for one another and say, "Enough is enough."

I was shocked to read that more than one hundred million women are missing worldwide!

How many women are missing in this country? Every year, at least another two million girls worldwide disappear because of gender discrimination. Thirty-nine thousand baby girls die annually in China because parents do not give them the same medical care and attention that boys receive. The results are that as many girls die unnecessarily every week in China as protesters died in the one incident at Tiananmen.

In India, "bride burning," to punish the woman for an inadequate dowry or to eliminate her so a man can remarry, takes place approximately once every two hours. It is estimated that approximately 5,000 women and girls have been doused in kerosene and set alight by family members or in-laws or seared with acid for perceived disobedience just in the last nine years. All this violence towards women rarely makes the news.

The book tells us modernization and technology can aggravate the discrimination. Since the 1990s the spread of ultrasound machines has allowed pregnant women to find out the sex of their fetuses and then get abortions if they are female. In China, one peasant raved about the new ultrasound machines, saying, "We don't have to have daughters anymore!"

Did you know it appears that more girls have been killed in the last fifty years, precisely because they were girls, than men were killed in all the battles of the twentieth century? More girls are killed in this routine "gendercide" in any one decade than people were slaughtered in all the genocides of the twentieth century.

There is an exploding movement of "social entrepreneurs" who offer new approaches to supporting women in the developing world. Social entrepreneurs are not content just to give a fish or to teach how to fish. They will not rest until they have revolutionized the fishing industry. After reading this book, I decided that I wanted to be a social entrepreneur.

Through their research, Kristof and WuDunn say, the

most effective contraception for girls is education. There is an African proverb that states, "You educate a boy and you're educating an individual, but if you educate a girl, you're educating an entire village." Educating women is the key to overcoming poverty and for overcoming war. But education does not come easy for women. One third of reported rapes of South African girls under the age of fifteen are committed by teachers.

There is no tool for development more effective than the empowerment of women. In the book, I read about an organization called "Women for Women International." It is a sponsorship organization that enables a person to support a particular woman in a needy country abroad.

Basically, you adopt a sister. You make a monthly donation of $27 of which $12 goes to a training program for the woman and other support efforts and $15 is given directly to the woman you pick. The managers coach the women to save, partly to build a habit of micro-savings and partly to have a cushion when they graduate from the program in a year's time. The women who are lucky enough to have sponsors go to morning classes that are devoted to vocational training to teach the women skills that will bring them an income for the rest of their lives. They also attend classes on health, literacy, and human rights, and one aim is to make women more assertive and less accepting of injustices.

The book makes a very valid point. There could be a powerful international women's rights movement if only philanthropists would donate as much to real women as to paintings and sculptures of women.

After reading this book, I knew I had to do something, so I contacted "Women for Women International" and asked if I could sponsor a sister, which I did. I am now on my fourth sister. My new sister lives in Nigeria. She is widowed and is caring for three children.

I honestly believe that it will be a woman who solves the many problems of Third World countries. Maybe it is one of the women that I'm helping to educate. Maybe it will be your sister. There are so many women who need your help right now. Next Mother's Day or for your birthday, do yourself a favour and pick up the book called "Half the Sky" and read it. Educate yourself about the issues that women around the world have to face every day. Then go to WomenForWomen.org and adopt a sister.

"You must be the change you wish to see in the world"
--Mahatma Gandhi.

THAT SOCIAL MEDIA OVERREACTION

This week I became Alice in Twitterland. I got sucked down the social media rabbit hole and ended up in the nonsensical world of Twitter-rants.

I am not proud of it.

I try hard to keep my social media feeds full of funny thoughts and memes. I pry my hands from the keyboard when things become too political because I know you cannot solve or help the world's problems in 140 characters. But this week I chased that White Rabbit down the hole and gulped from the bottle labelled "Drink Me" until I became as small as the rest.

I told a Monk off.

I told you I am not proud of my behaviour.

I made the mistake of thinking Twitter was like Facebook. Then I realized it was not. Twitter is the Wild West with outlaws and gunslingers and makes Facebook look like Downton Abbey.

My crime? I Tweeted, "For those who convict police officers without seeing or hearing facts from the investigation, Lord we pray @UnvirtuousAbbey"

It began an avalanche of hate Tweeted back at me. I had no idea what I did wrong. I really did not get it. I also posted it to Facebook and received nothing but love.

Apparently, you can support cops on Facebook but not on Twitter.

Anyone who knows me knows I am not a mean-spirited person. I do not take joy in anyone's pain. I am active in my church, all about family, and spend a lot of time helping charities. I try to be a nice person.

I am also the wife of a retired police officer and I am a retired civilian member of the Royal Canadian Mounted Police. During my career, fourteen of our members were murdered across this country. I lost track of how many died due to accidents or other means. Three I worked with committed suicide.

I know what it is like to get out of your car in the morning and look up to see the flag at half-mast, then wonder, "What happened overnight? Who is dead? Do I know them? Was it here?"

I know what it is like to sit through the funerals and memorial services and hear the muffled crying of those around you. I know what it is like to see a tear roll down the face of a man you thought was bulletproof, and feel the chill going up your spine when you know everyone in the room is thinking, "There but for the grace of God go I."

I know what it is like to get a call from the Communication Centre at 2:00 AM telling me my husband is in the Emergency Unit again. I know what it is like to watch your husband leave for work, then have your heart jump out of your body every time the phone rings or someone knocks on the door. As the wife of a police officer, you know you must be always ready for the worst. I know what it is like to tell kids, "You can open the big gifts as soon as Daddy gets home," or "I am sorry I missed your concert I just couldn't leave work."

I get passionate when it comes to standing up for police.

I made a simple statement that those in policing would understand... wait until the investigation is complete and then decide who is right and wrong. I was called racist, accused of praising murders, and interfering with the grieving process.

I did not know any of these people, but they felt entitled to spew their hate and anger towards me. I felt like deleting my Twitter account, felt deflated and attacked for days. It really affected me.

These people felt they had a right to say whatever they wanted on Twitter, but I did not. I think it is indicative of the world we live in. Where people feel they have a right to walk up to a police officer trying to do his/her job, hurl insults at them, and then record it on their phone so they can post it to social media to gain sympathy.

What if I went to their workplace and hurled insults at them, recorded it and posted it to my social media accounts.

That would be called harassment, wouldn't it?

The police are held to a higher standard. I know. But maybe the public should be held to a higher standard, too.

When it comes to issues and problems, there is a right way and a wrong way to solve and deal with them. Then there is that social media overreaction where every armchair critic in the world can hide behind their keyboards and belittle celebrities for being overweight, athletes who drop a ball, parents who look away for a second, and cops who are trying to do their job.

We all take a slug of that "Drink me" potion every now and again, making us too small.

I am not deleting my Twitter account. I am also not going to get caught up in the social media overreaction anymore.

It is a nonsensical world and a world I do not want to be part of.

A FAKE TAN IS LIKE FAKE BOOBS. EVERYBODY LAUGHS BEHIND YOUR BACK.

My friend Karen told me, "Brown fat is better than white fat any day," and I totally agree. So, before I head to a beach, I buy a tanning package.

I figure if I am ridiculously brown, I will blend in with the sand and no one will notice my muffin belly. Works like a charm. Until recently.

I went to a dermatologist. He told me that I am 100% at risk for skin cancer because of my tanning booth use!

"What? I don't abuse it!" Seriously, I don't. I go once or twice or three or four times a month to maintain a base coat and I go a little more if I am going down South and during Christmas, so I do not look too pasty in that low-cut party dress. But I do not abuse it. It is not like I'm going every day.

He gave me a stern talking to about how he just attended the funeral of a thirty-six-year-old patient who died of skin cancer and explained how I was playing Russian Roulette with my life. He ended it with "The 80's are over. Let them go!" That was harsh.

So began my quest to find the perfect self-tanner.

The problem with self-tanners is they are a lot like over-sized fake boobs. Once your back is turned, everyone will point at you and laugh but no one will tell you how ridiculous you look. Except your children.

My first self-tanner turned my bathroom in to a spray booth. It was the kind you sprayed all over your body and waited until it dried before you got dressed. It took a long time and left a thin film of orange all over my bathroom floor and walls. After ten minutes I was convinced it was dry, so I put on my pajamas. The next morning, I got out of the shower and could not wait to see my golden glow in the mirror. Except it was not the golden glow promised on the tin. I did not wait long enough for it to dry and it wasn't even. Now I looked like an orange zebra. I had to get back in the shower and scrub my stripes until they came off or bled.

I decided that I would retry the spray, but this time outdoors. I waited until dark and ran out in my backyard, where no one could see me. I dropped my housecoat and stood there in only underwear (ugly ones of course, I would not ruin a good pair). I sprayed myself from head to toe and figured the wind would dry me in a hurry, except that night there was no wind. So, I jumped up and down, trying to get the paint to dry. Hubby came to the backdoor, wondering why it was open so late at night, and almost locked me out.

I yelled, "Don't lock that door!" He looked out to see his mostly naked wife jumping up and down behind a tree in the backyard and all he said was, "Oh it's you. If this is another menopause thing, I am going to bed. I don't want to see how this one ends." It did not end well. The next day, in the bathroom light, I realized that the front of my legs were extremely brown. The backs were white. My arms were brown, but my chest and back were white. I looked like a menopausal panda bear. I spent another half hour in the shower trying to get back to my original colour.

Back to the drug store. I found a rub-in cream. That night I rubbed every inch of me with this "guaranteed natural tan" cream. When I got out of bed the next morning, I was shocked to see my shadow still laying there. The tanning cream had rubbed off my body, onto the white bed sheets. It had left a perfect outline of my body on the bed. It was like a tanning crime scene.

I was surprised that my tan was perfect. After my shower it looked even better. I was delighted with myself until later that day when my son asked if I was running for president. "What are you talking about?" I exclaimed. "You look like Donald Trump. You're orange." I looked towards hubby, who was trying desperately to avoid eye contact. "Am I orange? I am not. I look good right?" All I got was, "Oh no, the BBQ is on fire," and he ran out of the house. The BBQ was not even on.

I ran to the bathroom and looked in the mirror again.

Maybe I was a little orange. I had to think back over my day and who I met with. How many people were laughing at my big fake boobs, I mean orange tan?

It took a good three days to scrub the orange off. It took months to stop my kids from constantly reminding me about it.

After some research and lots of trial and error, I discovered St. Tropez Self Tan Luxe Dry Oil. It is about $50 at Shoppers Drug Mart. But spend the extra $10 and buy the application mitt to put it on right. It is a mousse that rubs in and the results are instant. It is so convincing that when I went back to my dermatologist, he started to lecture me again about tanning beds. He could not believe my colour was a fake bake.

There is nothing funny about cancer. I stopped smoking over twenty years ago because I did not want lung cancer, so I would be foolish to continue to use tanning beds after all the information that is available on them.

I still believe brown fat is better than white fat any day, except now my muffin belly is a painted-on brown. But the boobs... the boobs are real, so don't laugh.

STEALING HER RECYCLING
A SNAPSHOT OF LIFE

"I am calling the cops," she yelled over her shoulder. Her fingers holding open the blinds as she peeked through the slats. "It's theft. They're stealing people's property," she informed him.

He pulled his gaze away from the TV screen, toward his wife who was standing in front of the big bay window in their front room. He knew better than to argue with her once she got something in her mind.

"If I see them doing it next week, I am calling the cops." She pulled her fingers away from the blinds and walked back to the TV room. Her husband was in between watching his favourite show and snoozing during the commercials. "It really bugs me to see them getting away with it." He nodded in agreement, although he never really heard what she said. "You're not even listening to me!" she yelled. He jolted awake. "I am listening. I am listening. You're calling the police."

"It is theft, you know. People put their recycling out every week thinking the city garbage people are picking it up. They don't realize that those thieves are going around after dark taking the bottles and turning them in for money. I have seen them do it several times now."

"It's not really theft, dear. People are throwing it out. It is just garbage. Who cares as long as someone takes it?"

"Who cares?" she screamed at him. "Everyone cares! People go through a lot of trouble to sort their recycling and put it out. They wouldn't do it if they knew someone was stealing it and profiting from it."

"People don't really care," he sighed. "I am going to bed. I am exhausted and I have to get up early." He pulled himself out of his recliner and staggered to the bedroom. She sat back on the couch, fuming. "He has no backbone, that's the problem," she thought. This was clearly an issue she would take on by herself.

The next morning she stood in the big bay window watching her husband pull out of the driveway. She sipped her coffee while peering through the open blinds. She heard the screen door of the next-door neighbour's house slam close and saw her walking to the end of the driveway, holding two full green garbage bags. She slammed her cup on the coffee table, spilling some of its contents over the table. She did not take notice. She ran to the front door, grabbed the two blue bags of recycling, opened the door, and quickly walked to the end of the driveway. She anxiously darted her eyes over toward the house next door, hoping to see her neighbour. The screen door opened again, and the neighbour came out holding two blue recycling bags full of plastic bottles.

"Good morning!" she called, and the startled neighbour looked up and smiled. "Good morning," she called back. She was not losing this opportunity and broke into a jog toward the neighbour as if she had important news to share.

"Do you put out much recycling?" she inquired. "Not a lot," the neighbour responded. "Well, I just thought you should know that someone has been stealing the recycling bottles from our neighbourhood. I wrote down his licence plate number and I am going to call the police if I see him again. You can't trust these people you know," she spoke like an expert on the subject.

The neighbour looked at her watch, making it known she was on a time limit and had to get to work. She couldn't help but ask, "These people? Which people?"

The neighbour looked across the carefully manicured lawn and knew exactly what people she was talking about. People like she used to be growing up. Poor people.

"Well, he drives a beat up old pickup truck. I think it is dark blue or black. I'll find out for sure next week because I'll take a picture to show the police."

"The police?" the neighbour inquired. "Yes. It's theft," she informed her. "Don't you think the police have more important things to do?" She cocked her head to one side like a dog. "No, I don't. That is what they are there for. To protect our neighbourhoods. These people are turning that recycling in and making money off it."

The neighbour lifted her full blue bag of plastic bottles. "This whole bag wouldn't get you $2." Then she remembered something. "He's not stealing. The lady across the street knows him. He collects the bottles in the nighttime because he works during the day at Canadian Tire or Walmart or somewhere like that. He brings them to the recycling depot because he has a daughter who has a physical disability. I can't remember what kind but anyway, he is saving for a wheelchair for her."

"That's what government is for! He shouldn't be stealing from us." The neighbour was stunned. "It's stuff we throw out. He's trying to help his child the only way he knows how."

She locked eyes with her neighbour. "Stealing from us is the only way he knows how? That's why I don't want those kinds of people going around our neighbourhood at night when we are sleeping."

"Do you mean poor people or disabled people?" the neighbour challenged her. "You've obviously never been poor. If you have nothing better to do with your life than peek out through your blinds and spy on your neighbourhood, maybe you should find something productive to fill your life with."

She was appalled. How dare the neighbour talk to her like that. She had lived on this street for almost thirty years. She had seen four families live in the house next door. Each one more obnoxious than the last.

"I knew when I saw you moving in that you were no better than that crowd of hoodlums that moved out," she stomped toward her front door. This would upset her whole day. Maybe her whole week. She began to grind her teeth, thinking if her husband had supported her on this issue last night, she would not be having this conversation with the neighbour.

She decided he would hear about it tonight.

"Maybe you feel sorry for those people, but I don't," she yelled over her shoulder at her neighbour.

"Maybe you should look at those people and say, 'There but for the Grace of God go I'," the neighbour yelled back.

Imagine bringing God up to her, she thought. Sure, she ran the church. She was there every week giving money and her valuable time. Not too much though because you know it is never enough for those people. They always wanted more.

Besides, they never once thanked her in the Sunday bulletin for all the good work she does. She decided then and there to call the Church secretary that day and complain.

WHY ARE PEOPLE AFRAID TO SAY THE WORD SUICIDE?

They act like they are going to catch it if they say the word out loud. I have actually heard someone say "Don't tell anyone it was suicide. Tell them it was a heart attack, because if you say suicide it becomes an option for other people in the family who are seeking attention."

A week after my brother's fifty-sixth birthday, he came home, put out the garbage, went to the shed in his back yard, and hung himself. I asked my husband, a retired police officer, why he would put the garbage out. He simply said, "Tomorrow is garbage day."

Looking back, there were signs. Nothing big. Just little things. Nothing that would send up a suicide red flag. He suffered from anxiety and depression, then medicated with alcohol and drugs. I thought once we got through Christmas, he would be OK. I always thought if he were going to commit suicide it would be around Christmas.

Over the last two years I spent more time with my brother than I have in the past twenty because of a financial issue he had gotten himself into. I have learned that when a person suffers from depression and anxiety, and medicates with alcohol and drugs, they become an easy target for those who want to take advantage of them.

There was no shortage of people who wanted to take

advantage of him.

I have had people say to me, "Tell him to get his arse out of bed, get showered and shaved, get dressed and get himself together." My God, don't you think if a shower and shave could have eased his pain, he would do it ten times a day? Depression and anxiety cannot be cured with a shower and shave. It is only lipstick on a pig.

During the funeral, a friend dropped in on her way home from work to offer her condolences. She asked, "He was only fifty-six years old. Was it a heart attack?" I said, "No it was suicide." She looked at me and explained the parking lot was extremely busy and she was double-parked. She basically ran out of the funeral home. I thought, "That was odd."

Then another friend came by to offer her condolences. Once again, I was asked, "He was only fifty-six years old; did he have cancer?" "No," I said, "it was suicide." She said she was sorry, then turned around and left the funeral home.

It felt like because I said "suicide" his death was not good enough for everybody. If I had said "Heart attack" or "Cancer" I would have received more sympathy. I think some people still have the mindset that if a person commits suicide, they should be buried outside the graveyard fence.

I decided to take a different approach. The next time somebody offered their condolences and asked if he was sick, I would say, "Yes, he suffered for a long time." Then they would ask, "Was it cancer?" I would reply, "No, anxiety and depression." They would look at me very funny and say, "Oh," not wanting to ask the next question. So, I would follow up with, "He died of suicide." Then they would look at me with wide eyes and a mouth open, not knowing what to say.

Everyone is obviously uncomfortable or too embarrassed to say the word… suicide. You cannot catch it if you say the word. No one asks me how I am dealing with the loss like they ask other people who have lost loved ones to other diseases.

After my experience at the funeral home, I decided I would change my approach to how I treated people who lost a loved one to suicide. I would treat them like their loved one had suffered from a disease and died from it. Because they did! I would not turn on my heels and say, "I'm double-parked I must go." I will take their hand and say, "Would you like to talk?" It is like anything, I suppose. If you have not gone through it, you don't know how to react to it.

People think suicide is a cowardly act. They could not be further from the truth. It takes an enormous amount of courage to put a rope around your neck and jump off a bucket. I could not do it. At least I hope I could never do it. But then again, I am not going through the kind of anxiety and depression that my brother suffered from.

I wish I could answer the question: how do we stop people from committing suicide? I do not know.

I know over the past two years I did everything I possibly could to help him. Sometimes he welcomed the help, sometimes he did not.

I asked Father Mark Nichols, my parish priest at St. Mark's to give the sermon. He had never met my brother and asked to meet with me before the service. We talked about my brother's life for two hours and I told him the truth. I told him about the alcohol and drugs. I told him about the anxiety and depression. I told him about my frustration when I had to deal with him and the times I walked away because I could not take it anymore. There was no sense in lying to a priest.

During the sermon, he told the story of a friend of his who boarded a plane with his young child. During the flight, they experienced severe turbulence. The child became very frightened and started to cry. The father comforted the child until the turbulence stopped and then the child went back to playing. On the flight back from their vacation the child became very anxious when he had to board the plane and began to cry. People around them started looking. There were comments of, "What a spoiled child!" "Why can't you get him under control?" And of course, the angry stares and judgment.

The father just sat there with the child and rocked him, comforting him. Father Mark said, "The child's father knew how he got that way." The father knew it was a past experience that created the anxiety and made the child cry. He knew the best thing he could do for his son was ignore everyone around them and sit and comfort his child until he stopped crying. He then said, "God the Father knew how my brother got that way. And he was now in His arms, being comforted without judgment."

The story really stuck with me.

I knew it was true. Only God knew how he got that way. Only God could comfort him through his turbulent times. I will forever carry the loss of my brother in my heart, but I do take comfort knowing that he is in the arms of God, being comforted without judgment.

Even after going through the suicide of my brother, I still do not know why people do it. I guess it is the only way they can stop the pain.

I wish there was some enlightening advice I could pass on. But I learned nothing. Other than, if you have a loved one who suffers from anxiety and depression, remind yourself "God knows how he got that way," and comfort him without judgment.

WHO ARE YOU CALLING PLUS-SIZED?

I am a size twelve. Size ten on a good day. An eight a week before I go on vacation. A twelve to fourteen when I get back from vacation, but that is it. That is all my sizes.

I watch what I eat from Monday to Thursday. I eat ketchup chips like a woodchipper on Friday nights with a red wine, of course. On Saturday we BBQ steaks with fully loaded baked potatoes and wine to wash it down. That is usually followed by a Costco apple pie or Tuxedo Cake. Then Sunday morning I crawl back on my Weight Watchers scales and start all over again.

If it weren't for the weekends, I would be as skinny as a rake because I am really good all week. I watch what I eat, and type everything into the "My Fitness Pal" app on my iPhone. I walk the dog to get my steps in and I drink a bucket of water each day.

So, I believe I am doing all I can.

I know I am never going to be a size two and I do not care. I do not want to be a size two. I am five foot nine. If I were a size two, I would look like a coat hanger or like I was on heroin. I do not want to see my ribs when I put on a big wool sweater, and I certainly don't want friends telling me I have no arse!

I would like to be more toned, but I had back surgery

and that means I cannot do sit-ups. So, I will wear Spanx like everyone else.

I am okay with that.

But apparently the world is not.

I walked into a dress store, automatically turned to my left, and began looking at clothes. The sales lady called out, "Excuse me, miss. You're on the wrong side."

My first thought was, "Is this the drag queen side? What side do I look like I should be on? Maybe I am wearing too much makeup." The stuff that runs through my head... I am not good with confrontation!

"What size are you?" She smiled at me as she walked toward me. I felt obligated to tell her because I did not know what else to do. "Size ten," I lied. I am bloating and I know I cannot pull this off.

She squinted as she sized me up and down. "Your clothes are on the other side. This is the 'Plus girl' section. It's size fourteen and up."

There were two ladies flipping through the sales rack, watching my interaction with this sales lady, and I felt like saying, "Okay, I'll go, but can I take them, too. They are obviously a size eight." But I knew she would not buy it. They were clearly in the right section.

I walked over to "my" section and started shopping, but I felt bad for the two ladies left over on the other side of the store, probably wondering why they were not told to take a walk on the wild side.

Why can't clothes racks go from size two to twenty-two?

Why do we need two sides of a store?

Why isn't there a bathroom in the same section as the change rooms?

I do not know!

Did our mothers and grandmothers all agree at some point that the size zero to twelves will shop on the right and the size fourteen to twenty-twos will shop on the left?

I did not buy anything there. I went to another store. I was looking for a white blouse. I asked the sales lady in the next store if she had any plain white blouses.

"Are you a professional woman?" she inquired.

"No, I am amateur one. A broken one really. I leak," I confessed, to her astonishment, and just for fun I put on puppy dog eyes and locked stares with her while I let a little drool fall out of my mouth and roll down my chin.

She looked away first.

"We do have white blouses over here." She brought me to the rack and disappeared to the back room. I assume to update her Facebook status to let all her friends and family know about the crazy lady in the store.

What difference does it make if I am professional or not?

And what profession was she talking about? I was wearing my Hootchie Momma shorts with heels. But who is she to judge me?

We have so many labels to slap on ourselves! Is that a Michael Kors watch? Is that a Coach purse? Are you a size eight or an eighteen? Are you a professional woman or a minimum wage worker? I need to know if I should waste my time showing you our white blouses.

A guy once told me that if I lost weight, I would look good because I had a pretty face… I was eight months pregnant! They have not found his body yet.

The bottom line is, I am healthy, happy and I like who I am.

I also find it extremely hard not to laugh at people. I

am not perfect. Give me a break.

I do try not to judge. I really do. It is hard I know... You know... We all know. So, if I do judge, I do it in my head only or whisper it to hubby or my BFF Nancy and make them laugh. Then I sneak away so they look all "judgy" and I do not.

My point is, what harm was it to let me look through the plus section? I would have found my way out eventually. I cannot help but think, what if I was size fourteen and wandered into the two to twelve section? Would she have told me to go to the plus section? Because if she did, I would have grabbed a size ten jeans and stretched that fabric to the breaking point until I got every last celluloid dimple packed in. Then I would have strutted around like a rooster in that store.

I do not mind a sales lady giving me fashion advice and suggesting some things that would look good on me. But seriously, you do not know what my day was like. I go into stores because they are my happy place, and I cannot afford real therapy. I do not want stress. I definitely do not want to yell my size across a store.

Finally, for God's sake, can't we find a better label than "Plus Sized?" Why not "Womanly" "Under-Womanly" and "Over-Womanly." That sounds so much better.

Excuse me, miss! You are too over-womanly to shop here. I could be happy with that.

LOT TO BE SAID FOR OLD FRIENDS

My friend Nancy and I have been having an argument for over thirty years. Back in our teens, when the whole world was getting physical with Olivia Newton-John, Nancy and I decided to jump on the aerobics bandwagon and get fit.

We donned our spandex pants, rainbow coloured leg warmers, and went to an aerobics class that was being held in the basement of a church at the bottom of Long's Hill. It was sixty hard minutes of tough stretching, jumping, and aerobic moves. We looked like Lucille Ball and Ethel Mertz in a comedy routine from the "I Love Lucy" show. By the time it was over we could barely suck in the nicotine from our Du Maurier Lights.

Still in our sweaty spandex we began the long climb up Long's Hill towards home. Each step felt like we were dragging a fifty-pound weight behind us. Halfway up the hill a young boy on the opposite side of the street called out to us, "Hey fat ass!" Then ran off into a laneway, laughing.

Now I thought that was a horrible thing to say about Nancy. She had worked as hard as I did, and I told her straight out, "Don't listen to him. Your ass is not fat." "I know," she said, "Because he was talking to you."

Catching my breath from the climb and with sweat

running down my face I told her, "My butt is not fat. He's not talking to me." With a spite brewing in her eyes she said, "My butt is not fat. It's you he was talking about." So, for more than thirty years we have argued back and forth.

I feel sorry for Nancy, not being able to face the truth.

Was not her first time either. Growing up we would constantly sleep at each other's house. Nancy was lucky. She had a twin bed to herself. I had to share a double with my sister. We had a record player in my room and stacks of 45s and LPs.

One night we were playing record after record as loud as the volume button would turn. Doing all the latest dance moves on my bedroom floor kept making the records skip, even with pennies taped to the arm of the needle. So, we decided to jump up and down on top of the bed and see whose head could hit the stucco ceiling first.

"Saturday Night" by the Bay City Rollers was blaring through the speakers and our voices were keeping up. Our heads were just about hitting the stucco when we heard a crash and came flying down to the floor. A second later my mother came through the door. "Turn the music down. What was that bang?" She looked down to see the foot of the bed had hit the floor; the legs had cracked off. Nancy and I had fallen on our butts on top of the mattress.

I quickly assessed the situation. I was jumping at the head of the bed; she was jumping at the foot. "Nancy broke the bed, Mom." "I did not," she protested, "you were jumping, too!" "But my half didn't break." I do not think my mother really cared either way. She took the legs from under the head and put the box-spring and mattress on the floor. No more legs to worry about. But in my defence, it was broken on her side. Must have been her fat ass.

Nancy and I are like sisters. No, we are sisters. We squabble back and forth, then move on. She is the godmother to my son and was there for his birth. I had terrible back labour that went on for hours. My husband left to get a sandwich and Nancy stayed monitoring the heart beats. The beats were going up and down and began to get erratic. Before I knew it, the room was full of medical professionals. My husband got back just in time. I was ready to deliver. The doctor told us, "The umbilical cord is wrapped around his neck. Don't push." I was scared. She screamed from the bottom of the table, "If you push once more you will hang your child!" I went numb. It was the closest I have ever come to an out-of-body-experience. The room was a blur, my husband was standing next to me. Behind him I saw Nancy, crying, praying. Then I heard the baby cry.

He was a colicky baby. He cried for days on end. I did not know what to do with him. I cried, he cried. He never slept for more than an hour and I was sleep deprived. I could not get a cup of tea in peace. To shower, I had to bring him in the bathroom in his car seat and get a quick wash. Still, he cried.

Nancy was going to trades school at the time and finished every Friday at noon. She would come over, take my son, and let me get a nap, a shower, and a cup of tea in peace. I waited all week for Fridays. One Friday she called to say she would not be coming because she was going to a fellow student's birthday party at a downtown night club. I felt like a criminal on death row who just had her last hope taken away. I cried so hard I could barely say, "That's okay. You go on and have fun." At two o'clock that afternoon the front door opened and in walked Nancy. "What happened to the party?" "It was boring. Go get your shower." She took the baby for a walk. The pardon from the governor had come. I would live another day.

Over the years there have been too many stories to tell. When I was in my early twenties, I foolishly married the wrong man. She was the Maid of Honour. Nine months later it was over. I crawled back to my old bed in my mother's house. I stayed there for days. While gossips spread their rumours, Nancy came over. She got in bed, put her arm around me, and fell asleep.

Unable to say no to anyone, when a fellow at a dance would ask for her phone number, she would give them the phone number to the Mental Hospital. One time she was complaining that no one had asked her out in a while, so I said, "Phone the hospital and ask if they have any messages for you."

A few years ago, we joined yoga together. The stretching and strange poses made us giggle, but not as much as the guy in the short shorts with the tiny hole in the butt.

At the end of every class the yoga teacher would ask us all to lay on our backs and close our eyes. She would dim the lights and talk about our inner peace. Nancy, who knows that once I start to laugh, I cannot stop, would always reach over, and grab my hand and not let go. I would be snorting and shaking, trying to hold in the laughs, praying for the yogi to end the class. After a few weeks, I did not laugh. I smiled. I looked forward to laying on my back next to my best friend with our eyes closed, finding inner peace, holding hands. I found it comforting.

My mother said, "Show me your friends and I'll tell you what you are." I must be doing okay if anyone is judging me by her. Not everyone has a friendship that lasts over fifty years. Just this past Saturday night we outdanced twenty-five twelve-year-olds when the DJ played "YMCA" at my daughter's birthday party.

She did okay... for someone with a fat ass!

ABOUT THE AUTHOR

Helen C. Escott is an award winning, bestselling Canadian author.

Her crime thriller *Operation Vanished* was awarded a Silver Medal for Best Regional Fiction at the 24th annual Independent Publisher Book Awards. Her first novel, *Operation Wormwood,* was nominated for the Arthur Ellis Award for Best First Crime Novel in 2019. Both were listed in the Top 10 Local Bestsellers of 2019 for Chapters-Coles-Indigo. In September of 2020 she released her third novel, *Operation Wormwood – The Reckoning.*

In addition to her fiction work, she is the author of: *In Search of Adventure- 70 Years of the Royal Canadian Mounted Police in Newfoundland and Labrador,* culminating from two years of research and interviewing Veterans to create this comprehensive collection of personal stories.

I am Funny Like That is a collection of funny and thought-provoking short stories. Escott wrote it for people who go through life wondering "Am I the only one who thinks this way?" She says: Well, no, you are not. Lots of us think that way and laughing about it is how we cope.

Escott, a retired Civilian Member of the RCMP was the communications lead on high-profile events including the RCMP's NL response on the September 11th terrorist attacks. She wrote and implemented the Atlantic Region Communication Strategies to combat organized crime and outlaw biker gangs, created a Media Relations course and taught it in several provinces as well as at the Canadian Police College, Ottawa. She also served as a communications strategist at the 2010 Vancouver Olympics. Before joining the RCMP Escott worked in the media for 10 years.

In 2017, she was presented with the CLB Governor and Commandants Medallion in recognition of her achievements of excellence in volunteering and fundraising work, including creating the idea and concept for the Spirit of Newfoundland dinner theatre, "Where Once They Stood."

In 2019 she was presented with the Governor General's Sovereign's Medal for Volunteers.

Made in the USA
Columbia, SC
04 August 2021

42761181R00169